Volunteer Selection, Screening and Placement Procedures

Scott C. Stevenson, Editor

WILEY

978-1-118-69053-6   ISBN

978-1-118-70391-5   ISBN (online)

Volunteer Selection, Screening and Placement Procedures

66 Tips and Actions You Can Take
To Ensure The Best Volunteer Fit

Published by

Stevenson, Inc.

P.O. Box 4528 • Sioux City, Iowa • 51104

Phone 712.239.3010 • Fax 712.239.2166

www.stevensoninc.com

Volunteer Selection, Screening and Placement Procedures

66 Tips and Actions You Can Take To Ensure The Best Volunteer Fit

Table of Contents

Volunteer Selection, Screening and Placement Procedures

66 Tips and Actions You Can Take To Ensure The Best Volunteer Fit

Table of Contents

Volunteer Selection, Screening and Placement Procedures

66 Tips and Actions You Can Take To Ensure The Best Volunteer Fit

1. Tips for Recruiting, Preparing Advocacy Volunteers

Many nonprofits rely on volunteers to spread their message and shoulder advocacy duties. Melissa Walthers, policy coordinator with the Breast Cancer Fund (San Francisco, CA), shares some insights on how her organization is recruiting and training such advocacy volunteers.

How do you recruit individuals whose job it will be to educate or influence government officials?

"The Breast Cancer Fund has a vast network of volunteer advocates, known as our Strong Voices. The individuals are able to combine their personal stories of how breast cancer has affected them with our prevention message. We recruit volunteers through signature events, as well as our website, e-mail lists, social media and Webinars."

What might these volunteers do?

"Our volunteers advocate for the elimination of the environmental causes of breast cancer through in-person meetings with corporations and elected officials, as well as sending messages via e-mail, phone and social networking. Volunteers also disseminate our message through educational materials like tip cards. We view our Strong Voices as both educators and advocates."

What goes into training, educating and preparing individuals for this volunteer work?

"We have in-person trainings, as well as online Webinars that help individuals better understand how to speak about the evidence and solutions to limiting the effects of environmental toxins that may cause breast cancer. We also utilize large conferences and other public events as arenas to help educate volunteers on speaking to the public about our mission."

Source: Melissa Walthers, Policy Coordinator, Breast Cancer Fund, San Francisco, CA. E-mail: mwalthers@breastcancerfund.org

To help current volunteers take a more active role in recruiting others, make it official. Give them a title and spell out what they can do to help.

2. Volunteer Brochure Helpful for Narrowing Interest

Volunteers who pick up an Idaho Botanical Garden (Boise, ID) brochure not only receive a three-panel document that is filled with useful information about the nonprofit, but also they are given the opportunity to share their specific area of interest by completing the interest form included on one panel of the brochure.

Content not available in this edition

More than 500 of the nonprofit's current volunteers were recruited, in part, through the Volunteer Opportunities brochure, many of them at events such as educational symposia or flower and garden events.

The brochure offers detailed descriptions of the four primary volunteer positions, including garden volunteer, garden visitor services, special events volunteer and education program volunteers. The interest form included in the brochure encourages those interested to enroll as a volunteer on the spot by simply completing the form and turning it in to the nonprofit's volunteer coordinator, Karen Christeson. Areas of interest noted on the form are entered into the nonprofit's volunteer management system for quick reference when filling open positions.

For simple and immediate access to pertinent volunteering details, the brochure can be found in PDF format at www.idahobotanicalgarden.org/index.cfm?fuseaction=category.display&category_id=3.

Source: Karen Christeson, Volunteer Coordinator, Idaho Botanical Garden, Boise, ID. E-mail: Karen@idahobotanicalgarden.org

3. Boost Recruitment by Publicizing Your Volunteer Philosophy

FUSION, a Federal Way, WA-based nonprofit providing housing and support services to the homeless, is an all-volunteer organization. Needing a constant stream of new supporters to maintain mission-related work, officials use a formal volunteer philosophy (www.fusionfederalway.org/how-to-help/volunteer-philosophy) to assist volunteer recruitment efforts.

What goes into a volunteer philosophy? "Our mission statement has always been central to everything we do, and the volunteer philosophy is really an outgrowth of that," says Peggy LaPorte, founder. "Volunteers are the heart of our mission."

A philosophy statement can be used to set expectations and help prospective volunteers understand on what principles an organization was founded, says LaPorte. "It sets a tone for what an organization is all about, and explains how it and its volunteers will go about achieving their goals."

A volunteer philosophy is best developed by a board of directors, ideally with the input of an advisory council of community leaders and businesspeople, says LaPorte. She also says ensuring volunteers are treated with respect should be a top priority. "It's one of the most important ingredients in keeping an organization able to grow and sustain itself," she says. "If volunteers don't feel appreciated, they will walk away in an instant."

If you're interested in elements a volunteer philosophy might include, take a look at FUSION's published philosophy, shown at right.

Source: Peggy LaPorte, Founder, FUSION, Federal Way, WA. E-mail: laportepeggy@yahoo.com

Your mission statement can play an important role in attracting volunteers, who best fit your organization and its work.

Content not available in this edition

4. Help Start New Volunteer Off Right With Right Assignment

A great match of talent and job assignment can make for a great volunteer.

When interviewing new or prospective volunteers to determine appropriate assignments, asks questions such as these to best match their skills with organizational needs:

✓ With what age groups are you most comfortable?

✓ If you had to chose between doing research in a quiet room or serving as a greeter at a public function, which would you prefer and why?

✓ Which do you prefer — asking someone for something or being asked for something?

✓ Imagine having volunteered with our agency for one year. What would you have accomplished during that time and why?

5. Agencies Agree to Memorandum of Understanding

In addition to establishing guidelines for your volunteers, take steps to assure that the agencies they work with meet certain guidelines.

At Smith College (North Hampton, MA), each organization that recruits students agrees to and signs an online, Web-based agreement called the Memorandum of Understanding. The guidelines agencies must agree to include:

- The organization shall designate one individual to coordinate the volunteer program who will serve as a liaison between the Student Organizations of Smith (S.O.S.), the paid staff, the community and the volunteers.

- Written volunteer job descriptions are developed and made available to prospective volunteers. They shall be updated as necessary and shall include information on time commitment, necessary skills, actual duties, etc.

- Prospective volunteers are interviewed and screened promptly and assignments are made as quickly as possible. Volunteers not placed should be referred to the director at the S.O.S. office.

- Records, deemed appropriate by the agency, are kept on the individual volunteers.

- An orientation is conducted by the agency.

- Volunteers will be provided with appropriate training and supervision.

- A supervisor is appointed to work with the volunteer and clearly defined lines of communication are established. The agency shall develop effective methods of supervision to ensure the volunteer is supported. The supervisor will be in contact with the volunteer on a regular basis.

- The agency or program agrees that volunteers must be provided with a safe environment in which to work.

- Volunteers' contributions will be recognized via individual or other recognition methods.

- Recognition of services, both individually or as a group, shall be given in ways appropriate to the program.

- The agency will conduct evaluations as needed.

- The board of directors and the staff who support the utilization of volunteers as an integral part of the organization are kept fully informed about the program.

- All organizations must be incorporated as not-for-profit, tax exempt or must function under the umbrella of such an organization. The one exception is proprietor-owned nursing homes or health care centers which request volunteers to visit, to entertain or to assist with special activities for the direct benefit of the patients.

Source: Tiertza-Leah Schwartz, Director of Voluntary Services, Smith College, North Hampton, MA. E-mail: TSCHWART@smith.edu

If your organization partners with others, be sure you're in agreement on key issues by asking those agencies to sign an agreement.

6. Volunteer Photographers Provide Valued Services

You may have volunteers in your organization who love to take pictures and usually get excellent results. They may be willing to share their skills the next time you need a photographer at an event or presentation — but make sure you have a shared understanding of the situation. Keep these ideas in mind as you arrive at an agreement:

1. **Offer free admission and/or dinner.** A volunteer photographer may appreciate a complimentary ticket to an expensive fundraiser in exchange for his/her services. Give a clear briefing or provide a checklist of the shots you hope to get at the event.

2. **Be sure the time frame and location are convenient.** If significant travel is involved, work out a mileage reimbursement arrangement.

3. **Give your photographer credit.** If you use these photos in your publications or give them to the local press, be sure the photographer's name is clearly identified.

4. **Decide where the volunteer's skills are most needed.** The best volunteer photographer may already have plenty of other work to do at the event you want covered. Find a replacement rather than asking the person to do double duty.

5. **Provide film and pay developing costs (if film is used).** Ask the volunteer to save receipts, so you can reimburse him/her for related costs, or authorize use of your account with a photo shop.

Targeted selection/ placement procedures — Need volunteer photographers? Reach a mutual understanding before they begin their work.

7. Plan for Following Up on Background Check Rejections

If you require candidates to pass a background check before becoming volunteers for your organization, consider creating a plan for those volunteers who do not clear the background check.

Background checks can identify criminal behavior, evaluate for drug usage or check financial references. Due to data privacy protection laws, you may not learn the specific reason someone is being declined in a background check. If so, you will want to put into practice a system for dealing with those who are rejected.

Consider the following:

- Will your nonprofit eliminate all volunteer prospects that do not pass a background check? If so, create a form letter or dialogue that explains to candidates the reason behind the rejection of their volunteer assistance and provide them with the name of the entity that provided the background check. This will allow persons to follow up and clear discrepancies, if applicable.

- Taking into consideration the constituents you serve, would reassigning rejected volunteers to a monitored volunteer effort not dealing directly with constituents be fruitful for your nonprofit? Could these volunteers work on mailings or other supervised administrative tasks that do not directly influence vulnerable clients?

- Should you ask applicants to clear discrepancies in their background and resubmit their application after another check is conducted and cleared?

Have a plan of action for any would-be volunteers who don't cut the mustard following a background check.

Making a plan to handle rejected volunteer background checks will create a course of action that reflects the professionalism of your nonprofit and may allow you to utilize all volunteers who apply.

One last thought: If it's necessary to perform background checks on your volunteer applicants, you may consider signing on with a professional background screening service. Check with other nonprofits in your region for recommendations of exceptional screening services or check the National Association of Professional Background Screeners at www. napbs.com to find a list of screeners serving regional and national organizations.

8. Tips to Recruit and Retain the Best Volunteer Drivers

Volunteer drivers are an important volunteer resource for area communities. Volunteer drivers oftentimes assist transportation-dependent members of society by helping them run medical errands, by delivering meals or by transporting those in need for any other purpose.

At Tri-CAP Transit Connection & Volunteer Driver Program (Waite Park, MN), volunteer drivers are a critical component to the services they provide.

Linda Elfstrand, Tri-CAP transportation director, offers her tips on recruiting and retaining volunteer drivers:

Targeted selection/ placement procedures — follow these key steps in selecting and preparing volunteer drivers.

- Ask current drivers to recommend friends or family members; coordinate efforts with your local United Way or RSVP programs; post opportunities at your organization's website or post a classified ad in your local newspaper.
- Offer thorough training. Tri-CAP volunteers receive a three-hour initial orientation followed by a three-and-a-half-hour class on child passenger safety. Refresher training is offered in half-day in-service opportunities.
- Arm volunteers with information about how to handle unusual situations. Tri-CAP volunteer trainees are asked to consider various scenarios and how to properly respond. Examples can include a passenger asking to make extra stops or bring extra people not on the manifest, a passenger displaying inappropriate behavior during the trip, or a passenger sharing information about his/her home life such as abusive relationships.
- Offer an emergency number to volunteers. Also, encourage them to call the home office if questions come up on the road.
- Offer reimbursement benefits. Tri-CAP asks volunteer drivers to use their personal vehicles while driving, but reimburses drivers for their mileage. This benefit has allowed the organization to retain their trained volunteers.
- Include volunteer drivers in organization celebrations, regular office communications and special events.

Source: Linda Elfstrand, Transportation Director, Tri-CAP Transit Connection & Volunteer Driver Program, Waite Park, MN. E-mail: Linda.Elfstrand@tricap.org

9. Seek History Lovers to Care for Historical Documents, Artifacts

If your organization features historical items, look for volunteers with a passion for history.

The Kansas State Historical Society (KSHS), Topeka, KS, boasts a volunteer program of 300 persons.

Volunteer Coordinator Joy Brennan says volunteers learn to handle and portray history by working as archival assistants and archeology lab assistants at state-owned facilities throughout Kansas. Archival assistants organize paper collections and transcribe handwritten letters and manuscripts into digital text format while others work with patrons helping them with research, such as looking for an obituary on microfilm readers.

Archeology lab assistants clean, identify, research and record information on artifacts found in excavations throughout the state or donated to the historical society.

Finding historically minded volunteers suited to archival preservation doesn't have to be complicated, Brennan says. She shares three tips for doing so:

Targeted selection/ placement procedures — three places to look for historically minded volunteers.

1. Seek volunteers from history departments or museum studies programs at nearby higher education institutions and within your local high schools. Prepare a presentation for students and faculty to solicit their interest.

2. Tap into your local retired teachers' organizations to find volunteers with an educational background.

3. Tap local Rotary or church groups or Junior Leagues for possible volunteers.

Source: Joy Brennan, Volunteer Coordinator, Kansas State Historical Society, Topeka, KS. E-mail: jbrennan@kshs.org

10. Checklist Helps in Crafting a New Volunteer Position

Have you come to the conclusion that your organization could justify creating a new volunteer position?

If so, do your homework before asking your supervisors to approve the new position or recruiting volunteers to fill it.

Follow a planning checklist that ensures the new position has been considered thoroughly to reassure your superiors of its need and value and to enable new recruits to hit the ground running when they assume their duties.

A checklist such as the one shown here will help you justify the position and plan for its effective implementation.

New Position Checklist
- ☐ Job description
- ☐ Qualifications of position
- ☐ Amount of staff support required
- ☐ Training required
- ☐ Anticipated budget needs
- ☐ Method of recruitment
- ☐ Areas of sensitivity/confidentiality
- ☐ Set hours/days per week
- ☐ Project timeline
- ☐ Work is done on- or off-site
- ☐ Adequate workspace and conditions
- ☐ Description of goals and objectives for the position
- ☐ Relationship of position to other volunteer and staff positions
- ☐ Methods for monitoring/supervising the position
- ☐ Methods for evaluating the position and completed work

11. Dos and Don'ts for Defining Volunteer Roles

Creating a volunteer job description is the first step for assigning the correct person to any volunteer role. Recruiting volunteers under a general volunteer umbrella can lump too many individuals with varied backgrounds and skills into the same generic category.

Gather your volunteer management staff and ask the questions, "What do we want this volunteer to do?" and "Where is our greatest need?" These questions will advance your efforts to define volunteer roles within your nonprofit.

Follow this list of dos and don'ts when assigning volunteer job descriptions:

- ☐ Do set aside time within your management team to define volunteer objectives and specific roles.
- ☐ Don't take the task of setting volunteer roles lightly. Volunteers bring a breadth of skills and services to your organization, so it's important to treat this task as critical to your nonprofit.
- ☐ Do create a list of volunteer roles including a task sheet that details specific expectations about the role for the volunteer.
- ☐ Don't create a list of impossible expectations. Be realistic about the time allotted for each volunteer role and ensure that the expectations of the role fit the time frame. Creating an extensive list for a 10-hour-per-month volunteer role will only ensure a feeling of failure by the volunteer.
- ☐ Do list the skills the volunteer will need to successfully fulfill the role. Are computer skills, people skills or technological skills needed? If so, be sure to include as much detail about the required skill set as possible to avoid assigning the wrong volunteer to the role.
- ☐ Don't ask the volunteers to take on the slush pile of work that staff refuse to do. Expecting a volunteer to take on the least appealing work is a recipe for disaster.
- ☐ Do review the volunteer job descriptions to ensure that what has been determined among your volunteer management staff is reflected in the job descriptions. Also, ask current volunteers to review the volunteer job descriptions and offer their feedback.

To make the best placement of volunteers, begin with a position description.

12. Conduct the Right Check for the Right Position

Volunteer screening policies are essential aspects of organizational risk management, says Linda Graff, president of Linda Graff and Associates Inc. (Dundas, Ontario, Canada) and author of "Beyond Police Checks: The Definitive Volunteer and Employee Screening Guidebook." Here, Graff shares advice on building a screening program suited to your organization's volunteer opportunities.

What do nonprofits need to better understand about volunteer screening?

"That one size does not fit all. Screening should be determined by the demands, nature and responsibilities of any given position. An organization needs only basic contact information about a volunteer distributing Gatorade at a marathon, whereas a volunteer providing medical or financial services would need a much more thorough screening."

Do any screening trends span the great diversity of volunteer positions?

"In general, I would say there is too much emphasis on police and criminal checks, and not enough emphasis on identity verification and qualification checks — making sure people know how to write the code they say they do, know how to properly operate the equipment they say they do."

Do you feel any procedures are consistently underutilized?

"Nonprofits seriously underestimate the value of reference checks, in my opinion. The ultimate goal of screening is predicting future behavior, and one of the best indicators of that is past behavior. Reference checks ... when done well, can be very helpful."

When is in-house screening appropriate and when should third-party checking services be considered?

"Outside companies are not necessarily better or more thorough, but they can be contracted to go deeper and get more comprehensive information than an organization can do itself. I think the reason more organizations are turning to them is a recognition that appropriate screening takes time and involves hard costs. The decision of when to move out-of-house really depends on the capacity and skill of in-house screening personnel, the volume of volunteers you have and the drain of screening on staff time and resources."

Criminal and police checks often dominate discussions of volunteer screening. What role do/should these play?

"Because criminal checks are cumbersome and often relatively ineffective, they should be reserved for positions of trust involving one or more of the following situations: access to vulnerable populations, access to money or other valuables and access to confidential, private, personal or otherwise privileged information. But it's important to keep in mind that criminal record checks are not foolproof."

Many organizations worry that the hassle or intrusion of screening will turn off potential volunteers. What do you say to such concerns?

"This is a long-past myth that has simply been discredited. Most potential volunteers now recognize that if you are going to put people in a position of trust, you have a responsibility to ensure that they are trustworthy. The word is pretty much out on the street on that, and not too many people will be surprised or put off by screening anymore.

"More than that, though, people's response to screening depends on the way it is introduced and explained. If you have a disgruntled screener who feels like he is doing busy work, potential volunteers will naturally feel that their time is being wasted. If people understand the purpose of policies and why they are necessary, though, they will be much more patient with the process. When screening is explained well, the loss rate is very, very low."

Source: Linda Graff, President, Linda Graff and Associates Inc., Dundas, Ontario, Canada. E-mail: LL.GRAFF@sympatico.ca

13. Prepare Staff Before Placing Volunteers

Once staff members request volunteer assistance and you supply needed personnel, do staff know what to do at that point? When volunteers show up, will the staff member in charge support them in a way consistent with your expectations?

If you are going to supply departments with needed volunteers, it's important they accommodate those unpaid helpers in a professional manner. Here's how to help:

1. Insist that any personnel desiring volunteer assistance first participate in a brief workshop designed to show the dos and don'ts of working with volunteers.

2. When requests are made for volunteer assistance — and such requests should be encouraged — have a process in place that allows you to get all of the needed facts before enlisting help: How many volunteers will be required? What will they be expected to do? Who will be on hand to assist them or answer questions? What is the time frame of the assigned task(s)? Are there any special qualifications required?

3. If possible, check up on the volunteers to be sure everything is going as expected. In addition, be sure they know they can come to you if they have a problem or question that is not being addressed by the department for which they are working.

4. Have a system in place that allows you to survey both volunteers and staff as part of your evaluation of the completed project. Knowing perceptions of both staff and volunteers enables you to make needed improvements.

It's not just about preparing volunteers. The staff with whom they work need to be equally prepared.

14. Combine Background Checks to Save Time, Funds

Consider working with another volunteer organization to conduct volunteer background checks to save on costs and resources.

The Kalamazoo Valley Museum (Kalamazoo, MI) requires background checks on all of its volunteers as many work with young children who visit the museum to take part in the educational opportunities offered there. The museum, operated by the Kalamazoo Valley Community College (Kalamazoo, MI), seeks to develop cultural, historical and scientific literacy through innovative exhibits, special exhibitions, planetarium programs, educational programs and family events.

Working with the community college that operates the museum, all museum volunteers undergo a criminal background check prior to taking on duties.

The organizations use the same consent form, which saves on costs and clears persons who pass the criminal record checks to volunteer for the museum, college or both.

Source: Annette Hoppenworth, Programs Coordinator, Kalamazoo Valley Museum and Kalamazoo Valley Community College, Kalamazoo, MI. E-mail: ahoppenworth@kvcc.edu.

Potential volunteers at the Kalamazoo Valley Community College and Kalamazoo Valley Museum (both of Kalamazoo, MI), fill out this consent form, which allows officials at the organizations to perform a criminal record check before assigning them volunteer tasks.

Content not available in this edition

15. Five Top Questions to Ask During Volunteer Interviews

Be sure to ask these top five questions during a volunteer interview to gain the most insight from your candidate:

✓ Why is volunteering important to you?

✓ What role or volunteer position will make you feel most valuable and fulfilled in our organization?

✓ Once you become trained and have served in that volunteer role for a specified time, in what advancement opportunities are you interested?

✓ Use the tried-and-true interview question, "Where do you see yourself within our organization in five years?"

✓ Ask the potential volunteer what they know about the organization already and what their impressions are.

Evaluate your candidate's answers carefully and jot notes during the interview to refer to when making your final decision.

16. Attract Single Working Parents as Volunteers

Single working parents may wish to participate more actively in volunteer activities, but feel unable to do so because of family and career responsibilities. Take their special circumstances into consideration by using techniques such as these to provide opportunities for single working parents to help your cause:

1. **Recruit teen volunteers to babysit younger children.** Develop a group of youth who are old enough to babysit children during meetings. Reward them with certificates or recognition. Not only will they become familiar with your organization at an early age, but parents can attend to business knowing that responsible youth are nearby caring for and entertaining their little ones.

2. **Give volunteers some supplies for a home office.** Some volunteers may have time to offer once they have fed, bathed and put their children to bed. Later evening hours may be the best time for them to accomplish their tasks.

3. **Offer them jobs that involve their children.** When you need signs or posters created, envelopes stuffed or other routine but crucial tasks, see if the parent of an elementary or junior high-age child wants the task. Older children may be eager to help paint, draw, sort mailings and complete other simple duties.

4. **Keep meeting attendance requirements reasonable.** While many volunteer organizations have fairly strong attendance requirements, think of important jobs that don't require a great deal of committee interaction, so the parent won't have concerns about arrangements. Two or three times a year, plan a meeting that is casual enough or in a location that children may attend without disrupting business.

5. **Provide plenty of valuable contact with a knowledgeable liaison.** When an experienced committee chairperson or liaison can keep single parents updated on important developments, or agrees to be available as a mentor for those volunteers, fewer meetings are likely to be necessary.

6. **Develop a "grandparent" team to spend time with children.** Like many senior citizens' facilities have started grandparent programs with small children in churches or other organizations, see if older volunteers would like to have a story time or special activity with the children of your single volunteers that coincides with your group meetings.

7. **Write a press release about how you are helping single parents volunteer.** Once you have two or three plans established to accommodate single parents while they complete their assignments, write a press release telling media what those plans are and how they work.

Targeted selection/ placement procedures — there are some key actions you can take to better attract and accomodate single working parents..

17. Training, Supervision Key for Emotionally Difficult Tasks

Specialized training helps volunteers prepare to serve as advocates for abused and neglected children as Court Appointed Special Advocates (CASA).

Christina Harrison, CASA state director for the State of Delaware Family Court System (Wilmington, DE), says volunteers initially undergo 30 hours of training where they are equipped with information relating to child welfare. Each volunteer is assigned an attorney to provide legal advisement.

Ongoing supervision by the staff volunteer managers helps volunteers with their sometimes-challenging tasks. But the learning doesn't stop there.

CASA volunteers are required to undergo at least 12 hours of continuing education each year. To help the volunteers meet this requirement, the CASA program offers more than 40 hours of free specialized training to volunteers annually.

Also key to a successful relationship between volunteers and the emotionally challenging work is finding the right people for the job. Volunteers to the program must be at least 21 years old and pass a background screening to assure that the individual is free of child abuse, criminal and any other offense that could endanger the children, says Harrison.

The program also looks for a history with a child welfare agency as well as any current court involvement. "Since we are court ordered, in every case, we want to appear non-biased," she says.

Since cases generally last for one year, the volunteer applicant must also agree to serve for that amount of time.

Volunteers are recruited for the CASA program through radio, press releases, billboards, brochures, magazine and newspaper ads as well as trade shows and community events. The program also counts on its current volunteers to recruit family and friends.

Source: Christina Harrison, CASA State Director, State of Delaware Family Court, Wilmington, DE. E-mail: Christina.Harrison@state.de.us

CASA volunteers are required to meet strict background requirements and complete specialized training prior to placement.

18. Require and Check References to Protect Organization

If your volunteer application doesn't include a request for references, it should.

Asking volunteer applicants for names and contact information of persons to whom they are not related — and then touching base with those references — can prevent you from signing on a volunteer who could wreak havoc in your nonprofit.

Ask each new volunteer for at least three references and then call each one before assigning a volunteer position. Take notes about what you're told and look for inconsistencies among the information you're given by each reference. Treat your volunteer applicant as though he/she is applying for a new paid position within your nonprofit. Ask the same questions of references as you would if this were a new hire, and include notes of your conversations in the volunteer file.

If an applicant gets a negative review from one or more references, weigh your options carefully. Try the following:

- Simply decline the person's application and offer feedback based on your reference check.
- Fill the applicant in on anything negative that may have been brought up during reference review and ask that the volunteer address each item raised. If you're satisfied with the volunteer's response, invite him/her to join your nonprofit in a probationary fashion. Schedule a review when the probationary time expires.
- Ask the volunteer to help at a one-time event. Monitor that person closely during the event and if things go well, invite them to help at your next one-time event until a positive history is proven.

Know that reference checks are just one step in the volunteer applicant assessment process. Be sure to require background checks and other specific screenings to best protect your organization and those you serve.

Don't be shy about asking for references for certain volunteer positions.

19. Code of Conduct Sets Expectations

Volunteers at the Virginia Living Museum (Newport News, VA) sign a code of conduct before embarking on their roles as new volunteers.

"The primary purpose of the form is to outline expected behaviors before volunteers begin," says Shandran Thornburgh, volunteer services director, who carried over the form from a previous position when she began her post with the museum in 2003.

Thornburgh adds the form to application packets given to new volunteers, who complete the form prior to being asked for an interview.

"This sets the tone from the beginning," says Thornburgh. "We cover the points therein at the interview and at orientation, as well."

Source: Shandran Thornburgh, Volunteer Services Director, Virginia Living Museum, Newport News, VA. E-mail: volunteer@thevlm.org

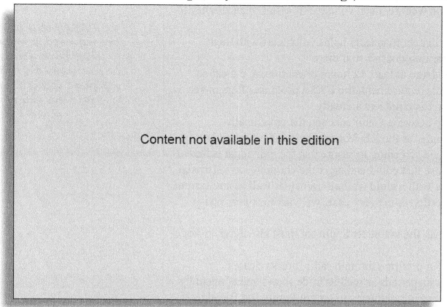

Content not available in this edition

Volunteers at the Virginia Living Museum (Newport News, VA) sign the code of conduct at left.

20. Questions Help Create School Volunteer Screening Policy

The more vulnerable a population is, the more important it is to screen its prospective volunteers, and few groups are more vulnerable than children. It is, therefore, vital for schools, both public and private, to have clear screening policies.

"The practice of background checks for school employees is standard issue for all employees with access to children. ... Why should this practice differ with school volunteers?" asks Bill Tate, president of HR Plus (Chicago, IL).

But easy as the decision to screen school volunteers might be, answering questions like what kinds of screening should be used and on what kinds of volunteers is difficult.

To help schools grappling with these issues, Tate offers the following questions:

Having a screening policy in place helps to determine the types of screening procedures you should follow with volunteers.

1. Does the school have a policy in place to ensure background screening for all employees of the school? Are teachers, crossing guards, teaching assistants, nurses, cafeteria workers, maintenance people — virtually all paid employees — screened?
2. What type of screening is conducted on employees? Is a national criminal background check conducted? Is the school conducting drug and alcohol testing?
3. Do you permit parents, grandparents and other family members to act as volunteers?
4. Do you permit non-familial persons (e.g., area residents, nannies, family friends) to act as volunteers?
5. Is there mandatory background screening for all school volunteers — whether they are family members or non-familial persons?

Some organizations worry that background screening will discourage volunteerism, but Tate says schools must understand that bigger issues are at stake, not the least being the possibility of the school being held responsible if a child is placed in danger by a volunteer.

"For the safety of the students, the parents' peace of mind and the fiscal health of the school, it makes sense to implement a comprehensive background screening program," he says.

Source: Bill Tate, President, HR Plus, Chicago, IL. E-mail: WTate@hrplus.com

21. Respect Volunteers Driven By Past Circumstances

Volunteers have many reasons for giving time and talents to your organization. Some will exhibit a strong sense of dedication and commitment that is worthy of special recognition.

By the time such volunteers have worked that selflessly and consistently, chances are you have come to know them quite well. You and other volunteers know that these individuals haven't always been so motivated or as fortunate as they are today, which makes them even more special.

In fact, some of the most dedicated volunteers are driven by a desire to right past mistakes or to keep from becoming too focused on tragic circumstances in their lives: A volunteer at a women's shelter may have been a victim of domestic abuse, or the person who spends every Thanksgiving serving in a soup kitchen may have once been homeless and hungry.

These volunteers who manage to think of others despite prior hardships should be thanked and honored in a special way. Their stories may inspire and encourage others who have been more fortunate to stretch a bit more.

However, getting past the traditional, glossier forms of recognition can be a balancing act. How much about their pasts do these special people care to reveal? Some will be candid and share their struggles openly, knowing others will be able to apply lessons learned to their own lives. Others may be driven by personal and private circumstances that they have not personally revealed to you or to anyone else — but that you sense may exist beneath the surface.

Following are considerations for honoring both types of individuals:

- **How much do you already know about the person?** Dedicated volunteers may be assigned to you for community service for crimes they committed, and you know the details. A mature and successful volunteer may be known to have been arrested as a youth. In some cases you will have facts, in others nothing more than hearsay. Yet they have worked hard and accomplished a great deal. As long as you can get the facts straight from the source, along with the volunteer's permission to use them, don't hesitate to use the information in a positive way.

- **Allow volunteers to speak for themselves.** When it's time for the reception to honor your heroes, help them write some remarks they wish to make without scripting the content. They may need your assistance in determining how many past details are relevant to the situation. It's your job to encourage them to speak only on issues they feel comfortable discussing — let them know not everything needs to be shared.

- **Is there a good human interest story for the media?** If your volunteers are the candid type, they may have an inspiring story about their recovery from alcoholism, family circumstances that drove them to become involved in your organization, or what keeps them going when they begin to tire. Reporters find these stories inspiring for other readers or viewers. The hottest fires forge the strongest steel, and people are attracted to those who have overcome adversity.

- **Be considerate of the volunteer's other family members.** Volunteers may be willing to share their lives and inspirations publicly, but discretion is important. If those difficulties involve living relatives, especially those locally known, be sure they, too, are comfortable with any mention of them that will be made.

- **Have quiet recognitions for those who value privacy.** Special volunteers may share experiences and motivations with you, but will never discuss them openly. They resist any attempt to recognize their progress and dedication — and mean it. You still wish to do something meaningful and special in their honor. Ask them what they will permit you to do. It may take some gentle prodding, but even the most reticent individuals will recognize an opportunity to continue their good work. The best honor for such people may mean making a donation in their name to a program or naming an ongoing program for them.

> *Some of the most dedicated volunteers are driven by a desire to right past mistakes or to keep from becoming too focused on tragic circumstances in their lives.*

22. Assigning Appropriate Roles to Senior Volunteers

As volunteer coordinator at Senior Services (Midland, MI), Carol Rumba works with seniors as both clients and volunteers. She offers tips for assigning volunteer roles to seniors:

- ❑ **Meet with senior volunteers one-on-one to discuss areas of interest and determine skill level.** Discuss prior volunteer and professional experiences to assign a role that best meets your needs and matches the volunteer's interests.
- ❑ **Perform necessary checks.** Rumba requires volunteers of all ages to pass a background check and driver's check to ensure client safety.
- ❑ **Have volunteers complete registration forms prior to their first service date.** Rumba asks all volunteers to complete a registration form in which they indicate areas of interest, which helps determine the best role for each volunteer.
- ❑ **Provide a learning grace period and thorough orientation.** Have new senior volunteers shadow experienced volunteers to see demands of specific volunteer roles. If the new volunteer finds the role too demanding, seek a more appropriate role.

Source: Carol Rumba, Volunteer Coordinator, Senior Services Midland County Council on Aging, Midland, MI. E-mail: crumba@mccoa.org

Targeted selection/ placement procedures — give your senior volunteers a learning grace period to help them develop a better understanding of their volunteering roles.

23. Make Sure Volunteers Understand Unique Challenges

Visitng homebound seniors is a service of great meaning to many older volunteers, but it also involves challenges that aren't everybody's cup of tea. Making sure volunteers know what they are getting into is especially important with this kind of position.

"If a volunteer is made aware of the exact volunteer opportunity, they are able to make an informed decision on whether or not visiting a homebound senior is for them," says Christina Ulloa, program manager for the RSVP (Retired Seniors and Volunteers Program) with the Doctors Medical Center Foundation (DMCF) in Modesto, CA.

Successful volunteers know exactly what will be expected of them and what they may run into while visiting homebound seniors. Potential issues they might face include the level of cleanliness, expired food, pets that may not have received proper care and suspicious neighbors.

"We want a volunteer to be prepared to walk into a home that maybe no one else has walked into for years," says Ulloa.

DMCF officials require volunteers to make a time commitment of at least 2 hours per month and be 55 or older. Ulloa says officials also ask about interests and past work history to better match volunteers with someone who may have similar interests. All volunteers also have to pass a background screening.

Ulloa and her team find volunteers by speaking at various events and venues, including senior info days, exercise groups, church groups or any other places where seniors congregate. It's also key to let other organizations know about the volunteer program, so they can help recruit participants. "We leave brochures at senior facilities, with the intent of family and friends seeing them and volunteering to visit others in the home while they are visiting their loved one," Ulloa says.

Once an interested volunteer has been identified, he or she goes through a multistep enrollment process that includes:

- Completing an enrollment form.
- Attending a training session (group setting or one-on-one) on basic first aid and identifying and reporting elder abuse.
- Passing a mini (in home) risk assessment once matched up with a client.

"If they are still willing to make the commitment, we send the volunteers to have their background checked," Ulloa says, "and once the clearance is given, we match them up with a homebound senior."

Source: Christina Ulloa, RSVP Program Manager, Doctors Medical Center Foundation, Modesto, CA. E-mail: culloa@dmcf.org

24. Make Background Check Policy Readily Available

While background checks may have become common practice in nonprofit organizations, volunteers may still be uncomfortable with the thought of having this probe into their background — as innocent as that background may be.

To help them understand the need for this procedure — and the fact that you perform background checks on everyone and are not singling them out — have documentation that outlines your policies and procedures. In addition to explaining why screenings are necessary and what is required of volunteers, include what positions necessitate a background check, as well as what would make an individual ineligible to volunteer.

Make this information readily available to all volunteers — current and prospective. One way to do this is to post your organization's policy online.

25. Surveys Used to Assign Roles, Evaluate Progress

Obtaining volunteer feedback via survey can offer your organization an opportunity to expedite volunteer assignments as well as evaluate the volunteer program as a whole.

At Children's Home Society & Family Services (CHSFS) of St. Paul, MN, group and individual online interest surveys are an important part of gauging volunteer interests and assessing volunteer experiences. Shannon Broderick, volunteer services coordinator of CHSFS, tells us more about how CHSFS utilizes its volunteer surveys:

How does the individual volunteer survey differ from the group volunteer interest survey?

"Many of the questions are similar as they have to do with the basics of timing, length of commitment and interest, but there are also questions relating to the make-up of a group such as the number of volunteers and age of the members of the group."

Once the interest surveys are completed, what's the next step in the process?

"The potential volunteer is contacted in a timely manner (typically within the week) by a member of our volunteer services team to discuss his/her interest and what we have available to assess if there is an opportunity that might be a good fit based on his/her skills, interests, experience, etc. If a possible fit is identified, the volunteer is then asked to begin the application process by completing a volunteer application. With individual volunteers, we also ask for references right away to ensure they can provide those contacts. Upon receipt of those two pieces, we contact the applicant to set up a time to meet."

What key questions are asked on the online volunteer surveys to help determine a good match for volunteering?

"Our survey is, for many people, the initial stage of the process. We ask questions about availability, area of interest and how long a commitment they're looking to make to help determine if there are any opportunities that could potentially be a good match. We also ask how they became aware of our work or if they have a previous relationship with our organization. We use that information internally as we consider our recruitment strategies."

The CHSFS website also contains a Volunteer Experience Survey ... How do you utilize that form? How do you go about addressing concerns raised?

"Interns and volunteers are sent the link to this survey at the completion of their volunteer experience and/or annually if they are a continuing volunteer. We use software that allows us to collectively evaluate the responses we get. If the volunteer expresses a concern or new ideas are shared, the feedback is discussed with the team on which the volunteer was placed. Our survey states that we intend to use the feedback to ensure positive and effective use of volunteers throughout the organization, and we do what we can to put their feedback to good use."

Source: Shannon Broderick, Volunteer Services Coordinator, Children's Home Society & Family Services, St. Paul, MN. E-mail: SBroderick@chsfs.org

The best volunteer placement decisions generally include seeking various forms of volunteer input first.

26. Make Volunteer Programs Outcome-oriented

Just as it's important to evaluate the effectiveness of all your organization's programs, it's equally important to measure those that are volunteer-driven to: 1) improve them, 2) affirm their effectiveness or 3) replace them.

Generally, each program should be evaluated annually and should measure outcomes on a quantitative and qualitative basis.

Here are some examples of outcomes you may wish to measure:

- **Individual and overall volunteer accomplishment toward stated objectives:** number of calls, amount raised, numbers served, contributed hours, etc.
- **Individual and overall volunteer satisfaction during the project:** attendance/absenteeism, results of volunteer satisfaction surveys, recognition, etc.
- **Effectiveness of volunteer recruitment:** comparative totals from year-to-year, number of new volunteers, volunteers per recruiter, recruitment structure, etc.
- **Effectiveness of volunteer retention:** comparative totals from year to year, changes in level of involvement/responsibility among volunteer veterans, etc.
- **Training effectiveness:** amount of time/materials committed to training, degree of staff involvement, level of volunteer understanding, etc.

To improve volunteer screening and placement procedures, it's important to regularly evaluate them.

27. Use Match Tool to Align Volunteers With Assignments

For two years, Big Brothers Big Sisters of Puget Sound (Seattle, WA) has been using a volunteer match tool to link volunteer interests with available opportunities. The Match Tool, developed in-house, takes would-be volunteers through a series of questions identifying their desired time commitment and desired activities or hobbies to guide them in an initial match that best suits volunteers' needs.

Rosalie Duryee, marketing coordinator for Big Brothers Big Sisters of Puget Sound, answers our questions about their success using Match Tool:

How has the Match Tool benefitted your organization?

"The tool gives prospective volunteers a good frame of reference for how they might fit into our organization based on their interests and available time. We don't monitor the tool's use, but it's possible that the match tool has caused some potential 'Bigs' to better understand the time commitment and opportunities to be involved with our organization."

Did you develop the tool or did an outside source do so? What tips might you share with another organization who is considering developing a Match Tool?

"We developed it ourselves. It's a series of Web pages linked to selection buttons. We looked at the characteristics of each of our programs, and then made a series of questions leading to the correct result. Our goal was to create a short and sweet opportunity, and to show our volunteers that being involved with Big Brothers Big Sisters is really easy."

How often has the Match Tool been used?

"Our Web reports indicate the first page of the match tool has had over 1,000 hits since January 2010. Each subsequent page has fewer views, but users are at least checking out the tool."

Would you recommend the use of a Match Tool for other volunteer organizations?

"Since we don't monitor the tool's use except to see how many people visit the Web page ... we can't say whether it's useful enough to recommend for other organizations. It is an asset to our website in that it provides another place to describe our programs and the opportunities available to prospective Big Brothers Big Sisters volunteers."

Source: Rosalie Duryee, Marketing Coordinator, Big Brothers Big Sisters of Puget Sound, Seattle, WA. E-mail: Rosalie.Duryee@bbbs.org

28. Tools to Help You Assess Your Volunteer Corps

When it comes to background checks, is your volunteer screening program stuck in the police-check-or-nothing frame of mind? Linda Graff, president of Linda Graff and Associates Inc. (Dundas, Ontario, Canada) and author of "Beyond Police Checks: The Definitive Volunteer and Employee Screening Guidebook," shares a range of tools guaranteed to help your screening efforts more closely match the position's responsibilities, shown at right.

Source: Linda Graff, President, Linda Graff and Associates Inc., Dundas, Ontario, Canada. E-mail: LL.GRAFF@sympatico.ca

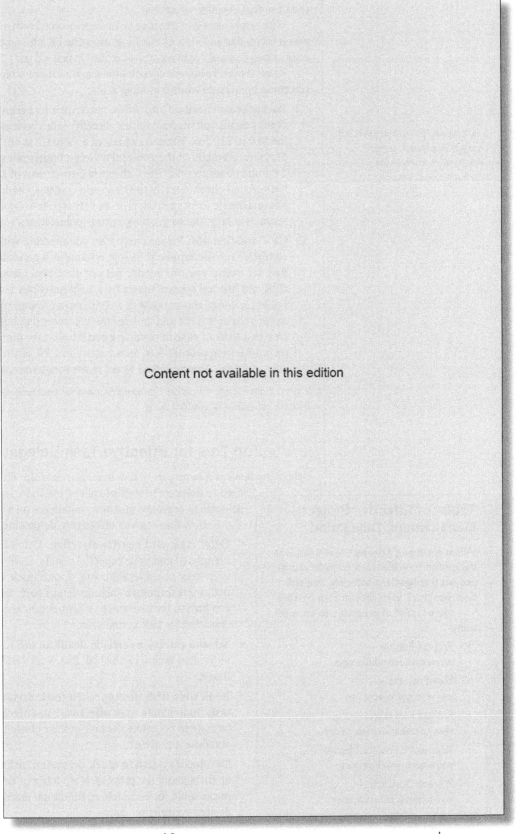

Content not available in this edition

29. Ensure Constituent Safety Through Volunteer Training

When serving its constituents — at-risk and underprivileged youth — Outdoor Outreach (San Diego, CA) puts safety first.

With nearly all of its 125 active volunteers involved with more than 250 trips a year with young clients that include rock climbing, mountain biking, snowboarding and surfing, the organization requires volunteers to be certified in first aid and CPR and pass a background check.

Katie Gangi, volunteer coordinator, explains these screenings and offers tips for screening volunteers while trimming costs:

Live scan fingerprinting is one method you can use to conduct background checks.

❏ **Background checks:** Outdoor Outreach uses live scan fingerprinting background checks on all volunteers working directly with youth and asks that volunteers pay the $10 to $20 fee. Volunteers present a valid ID at one of the numerous Live Scan providers throughout the area and undergo fingerprint scans to determine if they have a criminal background. The California Department of Justice sends results of the background check directly to Gangi and contacts Outdoor Outreach if a person who has undergone the screening process gets arrested. Learn more about fingerprinting services at http://ag.ca.gov/fingerprints/publications/contact.php.

❏ **CPR and first aid:** Persons may start volunteering without first-aid or CPR certification to determine if the opportunity is a good fit for them. After a few outings, they are strongly encouraged to get certified, says Gangi. Volunteers may attend CPR and first aid courses taught by a field instructor from Outdoor Outreach. Once a volunteer completes or updates a certification, Gangi places a copy of the certification in the volunteer's file and updates the volunteer database. On-site training, she notes, creates a level of ease in obtaining certification for the volunteer and creates a smooth record-keeping process. For information on CPR or first-aid trainers, Gangi suggests contacting the American Red Cross at www.redcross.org.

Source: Katie Gangi, Volunteer Coordinator, Outdoor Outreach, San Diego, CA.
E-mail: Katie@outdooroutreach.org

30. Top Tips for Effective Task Delegation

Delegating tasks is a large part of any management role. Volunteer managers not only need to delegate to staff members, but more importantly, need to effectively delegate to seasoned and new volunteers on a regular basis.

Follow these tips in effectively delegating tasks to volunteers:

Tools for Effective Project Management, Delegation

When managing a project which requires delegation to volunteers, consider using project management software that will help you track each project step-by-step.

Here's a list of programs to consider using:

- Project Bubble — www.projectbubble.com
- Easy Projects — www.easyprojects.net
- Project Kickstart — www.projectkickstart.com
- Teamwork Project Manager — www.teamworkpm.net
- Project On Click — www.projectonclick.com

- **Offer clear and concise direction.** Detail the task that needs to be completed and your expected results. Deliver your request in person and, whenever possible, follow up your request in writing via e-mail to ensure nothing is forgotten. Include details such as resources the individual can turn to for assistance or further guidance, and consider including a checklist for task completion.

- **Set and convey a realistic deadline** and solicit confirmation from the individual taking on the task that work can be completed within that time frame.

- **Be flexible with the approach the individual takes in completing the task.** Individuals work effectively in different ways, so offer volunteers the latitude to complete the task in their chosen manner as long as the desired outcome is reached.

- **Develop a system to track delegated tasks** allowing for follow-up throughout the process. Keep a log of delegated tasks, volunteers responsible for completion, follow-up dates and notes, along with the desired completion date.

31. Integrate Risk Management Measures in Handbook

When creating a volunteer handbook, don't forget to incorporate important risk management measures as a guide for your volunteers. Adding important risk management details will arm your volunteers with information on boundaries that should not be crossed and safeguard your nonprofit. Consider adding the following important risk management measures to protect your volunteers:

- As a volunteer, you must secure your own boundaries when working with a client or in the field. If you are feeling uncertain about a situation, ask before you act. Use your own best judgment, and don't be afraid to ask for clarification or help from your volunteer manager.
- Always travel with a fellow volunteer when working off-site.
- When working with children or clients who are members of the opposite sex, always be in the presence of another adult and/or volunteer team member.
- Do not share personal contact information with clients.
- Keep any information pertaining to clients confidential, including full names and medical conditions. There are confidentiality laws that pertain to certain information. Outline these in the volunteer manual.
- If you have any concerns regarding the safety or well-being of a client, please share this information with the service site supervisor.
- Be aware that you can decline to perform a task when you feel the request is inappropriate, beyond your skill level, or training level or if you perceive a situation to be unsafe physically or emotionally.

To help your volunteers know what they can and cannot do, eliminate any gray areas by spelling out procedures in your volunteer handbook and during training procedures.

32. Create Volunteer Manual to Streamline Process

Use your organization's staff manual as a basis from which to create one for volunteers.

"Our volunteer manual upholds the same expectations in terms of health and safety with the volunteers as the staff in the staff manual," says Becky Carlino, director of community engagement at the Western Reserve Historical Society (Cleveland, OH). "The volunteer handbook is an essential part of a fully functioning volunteer program. It provides clear guidelines with regard to expectations for work, relationships between volunteers and staff, and the rights and responsibilities of volunteers and staff when working together."

Working in tandem with the Forum for Volunteer Administrators (Cleveland, OH), an organization ensuring that similar organizations in the region follow the same protocol, Carlino organized her volunteer manual with the following headings (which may work for other nonprofits looking to create a volunteer manual):

- History and About the Organization — to include staff structure.
- Mission and Vision of the Organization.
- Volunteer Program Structure — outline who reports to whom.
- Volunteer Policy — topics include: Involvement, Service, Management Rights, Membership, Youth, Background Investigations, Training, Attendance, Dress Code, Conduct, Placement, Computer Use Policy.
- Company and Volunteer Policies — topics include: EEO Statement, Intellectual Property, Media, Telephone Usage.
- Company Safety Policy — topics should include: Safety Partnership, Unsafe Working Conditions, Safety Training, Drug Free Workplace, Smoking Policy, Violence in the Workplace, Visitors in Work Areas, No Weapons Policy.
- State and Federal Laws Regarding Volunteerism.
- Acknowledgement of Receipt and Volunteer's Copy of Acknowledgement form.

Source: Becky Carlino, Director of Community Engagement, Western Reserve Historical Society, Cleveland, OH. E-mail: bcarlino@wrhs.org

33. Signed Agreement Protects All Parties

Whether your organization has hundreds of volunteers offering their services or only a few volunteer board members, consider a signed agreement to protect the interest of your organization and your volunteers.

The Northwest Independent School District Education Foundation's (NEF) of Fort Worth, TX, 18 members of its volunteer board of directors are required to sign a board member agreement that outlines the roles and responsibilities of board members, as well as the foundation itself.

"An agreement between the volunteers and the NEF protects everyone's interest and gives clear direction for the expectations of both parties," says Marcia Schmitz, executive director.

Schmitz says this agreement, along with a completed interest form and the review of a board member fact sheet, are required at the beginning of each year or when the board member completes his or her orientation.

Source: Marcia Schmitz, Executive Director, Northwest Independent School District Education Foundation, Fort Worth, TX.
E-mail: mschmitz@nisdtx.org

This volunteer agreement for the Northwest Independent School District Education Foundation (Fort Worth, TX) features elements that could be used for other volunteer boards or individual volunteers.

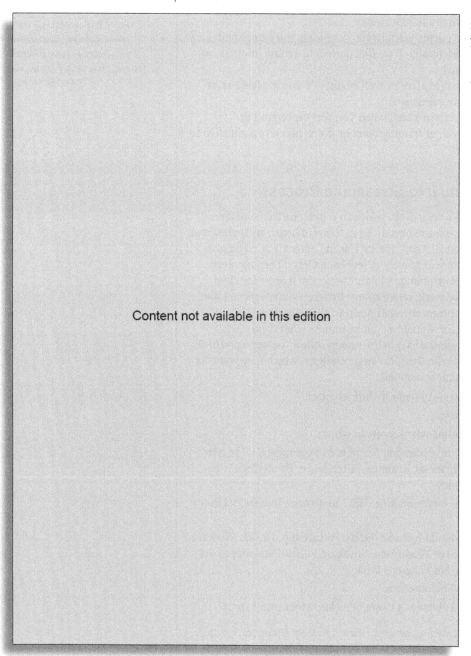

Content not available in this edition

34. Seek and Assign Volunteers With Writing Skills

Identifying volunteers with specific skills can offer your organization the opportunity to tap those skills for the betterment of your nonprofit.

Beth Upham, manager of volunteer services at the Morristown Memorial Hospital (Morristown, NJ), has identified three volunteers with keen writing and interviewing abilities and has focused their efforts on one specific project. These volunteers have been assigned to interview fellow Depression Era volunteers to capture their stories by recording their memories and service at the hospital.

Upham uses the information to feature volunteers in her newsletter. She has also created posters featuring the Depression Era volunteers and the interviews, using them at the annual volunteer luncheon and on the organization's website.

To manage a volunteer writing project and utilize the final interviews, Upham recommends:

- Obtaining permission from the volunteers who will be interviewed.
- Giving the volunteer writer contact information for the story subjects.
- Working with the volunteer writer to establish a deadline for his/her story.
- Offering the volunteer writer full credit for all published work as a benefit for working on the project.
- Sharing the published stories with staff. Hospital staff is always interested in learning more about the volunteers they interact with and see in the hallways.

Source: Beth Upham, Manager of Volunteer Services and Pastoral Care, Morristown Memorial Hospital, Morristown, NJ. E-mail: Beth.Upham@atlantichealth.org

Targeted selection/ placement procedures — spell out the details of writing projects for volunteers who offer their writing skills.

35. Proceed Slowly With Online Volunteer Descriptions

Becky Ricketts, community resource manager for SeniorCare Experts (Louisville, KY), says she grappled with the decision to post volunteer job descriptions on the organization's website.

Ricketts says she hesitated because of concern that including too much detail about volunteer roles could backfire, turning prospects away. So the organization first tested the idea to evaluate its effectiveness. The result is a website that is constantly being evaluated, and which currently features volunteer job descriptions for key positions, with duties described in encouraging terms.

If you haven't taken the leap to add volunteer job descriptions to your website, Ricketts suggests following these ideas for testing the concept:

- ❑ Consider only adding staple positions. Ricketts has decided to post only key volunteer position descriptions such as board member, meal delivery person and transport drivers at the site to test this approach to recruitment.

- ❑ Add key phrases on the volunteer description page to encourage volunteerism such as "Volunteering makes you happier!" or "Volunteering keeps you active and healthy."

- ❑ Track response from your Web page by asking applicants where they heard about volunteer posts. Evaluate responses monthly or quarterly to determine how posting job descriptions promotes volunteerism at your nonprofit.

- ❑ Ask new applicants who are responding to postings at your website pointed questions about the effectiveness of this idea. Obtain information from new volunteers to address issues or concerns about the clarity of the information posted and tweak as needed.

Source: Becky Ricketts, Community Resource Manager, SeniorCare Experts, Louisville, KY. E-mail: b.ricketts@srcareexperts.org

36. Clarify New Tasks Before Assigning Them

It pays to think through a new volunteer task before assigning it or even bringing it to the attention of others. By answering certain key questions, you can determine the type of volunteer needed for a project, the resources needed and much more.

Answer these key questions the next time you think of a new volunteer task:

1. What does the person need to know to complete the task?
2. What skills or volunteer traits would be particularly helpful in completing the task?
3. What level of internal support and supervision will be required?
4. Over what time period would the task be completed? Is there a deadline date?
5. Are there certain work environment restrictions regarding the task?
6. How many individuals will be required to satisfactorily complete the task, and how will they be recruited?
7. How much time will be required of each volunteer (e.g., estimated number of hours)?
8. What financial resources will be needed to complete the task?
9. Does the completed task call for follow-up or evaluation? How so?
10. Would this task be repeated in the future? How often and when?

37. Have Volunteers Sign a Code of Conduct

The way volunteers behave while serving your organization in public has a big impact on how the organization is perceived. Having volunteers sign a code of conduct agreement can protect you legally and set a precedent that excellent performance is expected. Blanche Hudon, Director of Volunteer Services for the Central North Carolina Chapter of the American Red Cross, answers the following about codes of conduct:

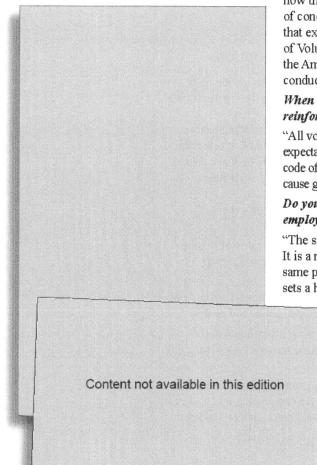

Content not available in this edition

When do volunteers sign the code of conduct, and how do you reinforce good behavior?

"All volunteers attend an orientation. During this time we clarify expectations, provide training, answer questions and have them sign the code of conduct. You can't just assume that signing a piece of paper will cause good behavior, so training is important."

Do you use the same code of conduct for volunteers and employees, or are they different?

"The same code of conduct is used for both staff and volunteers. It is a national policy implemented by all local chapters. Using the same policy shows volunteers how important their service is and sets a high standard for behavior."

What topics does the code of conduct cover?

"It is a thorough document that covers prohibited behaviors, such as not using the name and logo of American Red Cross for personal use, accepting or seeking financial advantage, confidentiality, promoting politics or religious matters not in conformity with the official position of American Red Cross, retaliation, and acting in any manner not in the best interest of American Red Cross."

Source: Blanche Hudon, Director of Volunteer Services, American Red Cross, Central North Carolina Chapter, Durham, NC. E-mail: hudonb@usa.redcross.org

38. Job Descriptions Formalize Roles Volunteers Play

Formal volunteer duty descriptions, like paid job descriptions, can help determine whom you are looking for, how those persons will be expected to perform, what is and is not acceptable and how to handle issues with problem volunteers.

To put volunteer job descriptions in place, consider the following questions:

- ❑ **What does the volunteer do?** Outline expected tasks in detail.

- ❑ **What is the level of commitment?** How many hours will the volunteer be expected to donate per week/month/year? Is there a minimum level of service?

- ❑ **What does the volunteer need to do to become a volunteer?** What does the volunteer need to do to remain a volunteer? Make sure to outline what will be expected of the volunteer in terms of training and paperwork.

- ❑ **What are your organization's priorities for keeping volunteers?** Your policies state all volunteers need to receive 10 hours of ongoing training a year. What happens if they don't? How will your organization respond? If there are no consequences for not maintaining requirements, does it make sense to include them? Such items could be listed elsewhere as suggestions or recommendations rather than requirements.

- ❑ **Do you need additional guidelines for specific campaigns or events?** For example, you may not want large groups to sell raffle tickets at your county fair booth because there is not enough room there or not enough for each person to do. It may be appropriate to set that expectation now.

Answering these questions will get you started on formalizing the roles volunteers play at your organization.

How to Create Effective Volunteer Job Descriptions

The first step in finding the most suitable volunteer candidate for your open position is to write a clear, concise volunteer job description. Follow these steps when creating an effective volunteer job description for your next opening:

Step 1: **Name the job.** It's important to have a defined name for the volunteer position. This will lend itself to better communication between departments within your nonprofit and give volunteers a clear sense of purpose. Adding a title for the volunteer position will also promote a sense of ownership for the volunteer member.

Step 2: **Detail the duties and role.** It's crucial that you take the time to properly highlight the actual duties required for the volunteer to best fill the position.

Step 3: **Create a time line** for service to include the time expected to complete the role and the length of commitment necessary to fulfill the volunteer position each week. This clarification allows volunteers to properly plan for assignments.

Step 4: **Spell out confidentiality expectations of the nonprofit.** Stress, on paper and verbally, the need to adhere to strict confidentiality regarding your organization and your clients.

Step 5: **Discuss the review process.** Outline in the job description what type of review process takes place in your organization and review timeline. Include information about the consequences of tardiness, absenteeism and negligent behavior.

Step 6: **Add space for comments and signature of acknowledgement.** Include an area where discussion points can be noted should adjustments be made for individual volunteers such as number of hours agreed upon or to jot down hours the volunteer has agreed to complete. Include a line for volunteer signature and date.

Step 7: **Add a list of immediate contacts** in the organization and whom to contact if tardy/absent.

Volunteer job descriptions create a specific outline of expectations by the nonprofit and commitment level required to best complete the job. When communication is clear at the forefront, the outcome is a committed volunteer with a clear sense of purpose.

Pre-placement interviews show would-be volunteers that you're serious about their placement in your organization.

39. Use Interview to Identify Highly Effective Volunteers

Finding a volunteer best suited for your organization is of utmost importance to sustaining the level of service your organization provides. When interviewing your next volunteer candidate, ask the candidate to provide the following examples to identify if he or she is a good fit for your nonprofit:

1. Can you provide an example of how using a positive attitude helped you overcome an obstacle?

2. Please identify three things about which you are most passionate. Listen for answers that make you feel confident this individual is right for your volunteer opportunity.

3. Have you had punctuality problems in the past? If so, explain.

4. Is there ever a time when it's OK to not show up for your scheduled volunteer time? If yes, please explain. Based on the answer, use this time to explain expectations and the consequences of not showing up for volunteer service.

5. On a scale of 1 to 10, please describe your level of commitment to this organization and give the reason(s) why.

40. Background Check Services Assess Volunteer Candidates

Applicant screening is central to the effective and safe functioning of any volunteer program. Application forms, interviews and training sessions are all part of this process, but formal background checks may be required, as well.

If your organization has reached a point where background checks might be more effectively contracted out to a third party supplier, consider the services below.

- **www.proformascreening.com/industries/background-screening-nonprofits.php** — Proforma Screening Solutions (Prucellville, VA) offers background screening, criminal record searches, verifications, personal searches and drug screening.

- **www.usabackgroundsearch.com/Pages/services_volunteer.html** — The volunteer and nonprofit division of USA Background Check (Ames, IA) supplies county and state criminal record checks, national background checks, social security/name/address trace, global terrorist watch/FBI most-wanted lists, sexual offender search, vehicle report, employment verification and professional reference verification.

- **www.lexisnexis.com/risk/nonprofit/bkgrnd_check_solutions.html** — LexisNexis Screening Solutions (Albany, NY) provides national, regional and state database searches; federal and county courthouse searches; social security number, employment, education and professional license verifications; motor vehicle reports, credit checks, and reference checks.

- **www.intellicorp.net/marketing/Screening_Services_Nonprofit.aspx** — The nonprofit wing of Intellicorp (Beachwood, OH) conducts criminal background and sex offender registry checks, employment verification, education verification, social security number verification and motor vehicle reports.

- **www.mybackgroundcheck.com/Business/Volunteer/** — In addition to standard background check services, MyBackgroundCheck.com (Redding, CA) provides volunteers with an online account to manage personal information and use check results for employment opportunities, rental applications and school enrollment.

- **www.backgroundchecksforvolunteers.com/** — True Hire (Uniontown, OH) offers basic, standard, expanded and custom packages, allowing nonprofits to purchase only those services they need, at a special nonprofit rate.

Sometimes it makes more sense to outsource background checking procedures.

41. Say 'No' Nicely to Avoid Turning Volunteers Away

Believe it or not, some volunteer roles are so popular that organizations run out of openings. Nice problem to have, right?

When you have more than enough volunteers on board for a specific event or task, how do you gracefully tell people, "Thanks, but no thanks," without turning them off from future volunteer opportunities with your cause?

Here are two tips for doing so:

- ❑ **First off, always be honest.** If the reason you have to say "no" is because you have too many volunteers for one specific role or task, say so. Frame it in positive terms, such as, "We are fortunate that so many people want to help. We've had an overwhelming response. We just can't accept any more volunteers right now."
- ❑ Next, **direct them to another appropriate role** and offer to keep their contact information on file in case circumstances should change.

42. Steps for Screening Prospects Prior to Interviewing Them

Ever feel like your volunteer screening process isn't everything it could be? Here two volunteer professionals share a few tips you might find useful.

- ✓ **Clarify what you do and what prospective volunteers will do.**
  Because people may have differing impressions of an organization's mission, help prospective volunteers understand the duties they would be performing. "People come to our United Way because they identify us as a place that helps people. We do help people ... (but) this is different from other organizations that provide more face-to-face services," says Becky Nahvi, volunteer center and community impact specialist at the United Way of Olmsted County (Rochester, MN). "Someone who comes to us wanting to work with youth might be better suited for The Boys and Girls Club."
- ✓ **Share with prospective volunteers any potential risks involved.**
  This can be something as simple as working on a ladder. "You should be clear and upfront about any, however unlikely, worst-case scenarios they could encounter," Nahvi says.
- ✓ **Create an application that provides ample information about a prospect.**
  "It should help you get a better understanding of a volunteer's skill set, interests, commitment level, professional and volunteer experience," Nahvi says.
- ✓ **Get responses from references.**
  "It's just like if you were applying for a job," says Jody Weyers, regional volunteer director of the American Red Cross of Northeast Wisconsin (Green Bay, WI). "We hope references will be honest and share if they don't think the person is a good fit for a particular area. That's very helpful. It helps us place them more accurately."
- ✓ **Consider making it a challenge.**
  You may want to have the process of becoming a volunteer require considerable time and thought. For example, Red Cross volunteers are required to fill out an application, read the code of business ethics and code of conduct, submit references and submit to a background check. "Because most of our opportunities are long-term and require a lot of training, we want people who are willing to commit to us, and a little more lengthy application process helps encourage that," Weyers says.
- ✓ **Share your code of conduct, and expect volunteers to understand it.**
  Things like conflicts of interest are important to make clear, says Weyers. While this may seem a no-brainer, explaining it helps make it clear, and highlights that your organization is paying attention to details.

Sources: Becky Nahvi, Volunteer Center and Community Impact Specialist, United Way of Olmsted County, Rochester, MN. E-mail: beckyn@uwolmsted.org
Jody Weyers, Regional Volunteer Director of the American Red Cross of Northeast Wisconsin, Green Bay, WI. E-mail: weyersj@arclakeland.org

Sometimes it may be in your best interest to require more time and thought of would-be volunteers prior to their selection and placement.

43. Checklist Helps Potential Volunteers Cover Bases

Having a clear cut list of items and tasks that potential volunteers must provide before being placed — everything from references to IDs to immunizations — can help save time and resources.

For many years the University of Michigan Health System (Ann Arbor, MI) has required all potential volunteers to complete a checklist of tasks. The Health System uses more than 1,600 volunteers at any given time and recruits new volunteers only three times a year. "It's very competitive to get a volunteer placement within the Health System. Having a clear-cut checklist makes the process much more efficient, because if they don't bring the required materials to their interview, it can delay the process," says Director of Volunteer Services, Alfreda Rooks.

What should be included on the checklist? Rooks says to look closely at what groups will most likely be volunteering with your organization. For example, with college students it's important to require a class schedule, so you know exactly when they will be available. High school students need a work permit from their school, and a legal guardian needs to accompany them to their interview.

The health system's checklist also includes immunization documentation, two references, forms of ID and authorizations for background checks. It is updated to reflect changing requirements as needed. If a potential volunteer doesn't bring all the items on the checklist to their one-on-one interview, they forfeit their appointment. The potential volunteer will then be placed on a waiting list.

Because it's critical to give potential volunteers ample time to gather all the required information, the checklist is posted on the hospital's website (www.med.umich.edu/volunteer/images/Volunteer-Information-Checklist.pdf). Depending on the list, Rooks says the process can take up to several weeks.

She also advises patience, noting that when the Volunteer Services Department first began using the checklist, it took about four cycles of volunteer recruitment before most potential volunteers came to their one-on-one interview appointment with all the required materials.

Source: Alfreda Rooks, Director of Volunteer Services, University of Michigan Health System, Ann Arbor, MI. E-mail: arooks@umich.edu

Do you have a checklist of steps or tasks that must be completed prior to a volunteer's placement?

44. How to Find Sign Language Volunteers

Volunteers who are adept at translating for the hearing impaired can offer your nonprofit and its constituents an even deeper level of service. Signing volunteers not only open your nonprofit's doors to a new segment of your community, they could also allow you to hire hearing impaired staff members to integrate more diversity into your organization.

Finding volunteers with the specialized skill of signing need not be complicated, try these tips for accessing skilled signers within your region:

- **Check with your community education services** to determine if signing classes are offered, then solicit the volunteer service of graduates. Additionally, connect with community education leaders to offer signing classes within your nonprofit to educate existing volunteers and staff members.

- **Find the nearest school for the hearing impaired** and contact the administrator to post your volunteer needs within the school and with the parent population. A list of global schools for the deaf can be found online at http://www.deafconnect.com/deaf/school.html.

- **Contact deaf and hard-of-hearing organizations** and ask to post your volunteer needs with their members. Go to the Library Services for the Deaf and Hard of Hearing to find national organizations at http://www.tndeaflibrary.nashville.gov/webnational.htm.

45. Find the Hidden Talents Among Your Volunteers

Recruiting an unskilled volunteer force to help out at a one-time special event is often much easier than finding certain professionals whose specific skill sets align with just what you need to help your organization grow. How should your recruiting efforts differ from one type of volunteer to the other?

Jennifer Iscol, director of North Bay Celiacs (Santa Rosa, CA), which offers support to persons with celiac disease and gluten intolerance, discusses the different recruitment methods her organization employs to attract all levels of volunteers:

How does your recruitment of highly skilled, executive-level professionals differ from the ways you recruit other volunteers to man special events?

"For special events, I just put out an e-mail to our general membership and take the volunteers who respond. Sometimes they show up, and sometimes they don't — but a few will really surprise me with their dedication and hard work. Those folks I may then attempt to get to know better by e-mail or in person at our events. I observe their communication style, skills and professionalism. When I feel confident that someone might make a good match for our needs, I'll approach him or her by e-mail to begin a discussion."

Are there tricks you've developed to figure out the hidden talents of as many of your volunteers as possible?

"Talented people rarely jump right in and offer themselves up. They become a member, observe our organization and my leadership skills, and slowly reveal more about their own skills and how they might contribute. It can take a few months or even a few years for them to come forward and accept a serious organizational role.

"As for their not-so-hidden talents, I find those using Google. I Google all of our new members for a variety of reasons, including safety. Sometimes I find that they are in a profession that would be a good match for our needs. From there, it's a matter of approaching them appropriately and respectfully, but usually waiting until they offer a bit of information about themselves. Of course, if they use their business name, title, website, etc. in their correspondence, then I feel that asking about their profession and volunteer interests are fair game."

How do you learn what potentially important contacts a volunteer has without coming across like you're only interested in a volunteer for the people he/she may know?

"People with great contacts are going to reveal themselves slowly after they've established trust. I don't know any way to shortcut this process without becoming a person I don't want to be!"

What's the most successful way to approach a volunteer with requests for his or her time, expertise, skills, contacts, etc.?

"If I can explain with enthusiasm and honesty how we would love to have them join our volunteer efforts, and how their particular skills would be helpful, they almost always respond in a positive way, even if they cannot help at that time. It's also all about contacting or talking with them directly. People are more likely to ignore a group e-mail and less likely to decline a personal request by phone or e-mail."

Source: Jennifer Iscol, Director, North Bay Celiacs, Santa Rosa, CA. E-mail: info@northbayceliacs.org

Your recruitment methods should vary depending on the types of volunteer positions you hope to fill.

46. Tap Volunteer Expertise With Pro Bono Consultant Program

Encouraging persons to share their professional expertise to benefit your organization on a volunteer or pro bono basis could save your organization hundreds or even thousands of dollars each year.

Oftentimes when you think of such pro bono services, legal work comes to mind. But Michelle Birnbaum, the pro bono consultant program coordinator at the Montgomery County Volunteer Center (Rockville, MD), says legal work is just a small part of the pro bono services people are willing to donate. "If you can think of a consulting service, there is usually pro bono work available," she says.

Pro bono consulting services can include:

- Accounting
- Information technology (website redesign, graphic design)
- Marketing
- Grant writing
- Fundraising
- Organizational management
- Social media marketing
- Budgeting
- Human resource projects
- Program evaluation

Birnbaum says that when representatives of nonprofit organizations approach her with project requests in the hopes of engaging a consultant on a pro bono basis, she works to match those requests with pro bono consultants who have come to the volunteer center. In doing so, she says, she has learned it is important to make sure the staff and board of the nonprofit organization are trained and ready to work with a consultant.

"In order for it to work, everyone needs to be open to consultant work," says Birnbaum. "The nonprofit world and the business world are very different. It's a bit of a culture shock. We want to make sure the groundwork is laid before the consultant takes on the project. If the nonprofit board and staff aren't willing to listen to, or go forward with, what the consultant suggests, the project will likely not be successful."

Birnbaum says professionals are usually willing to commit to 30-, 60- or 90-day projects. "We don't solicit projects that are expected to last longer than three months," she says. "Whether it's a website redesign, marketing or grant writing activity, most of these volunteers are looking for short-term, well-defined projects where they can make a significant impact."

To seek out persons to donate professional services, Birnbaum says, "Reach out within your network. You'll be amazed at what people will donate. Don't be afraid to ask for more than just raffle prizes. Ask for in-kind services, as well."

Source: Michelle Birnbaum, Pro Bono Consultant Coordinator, Montgomery County Volunteer Center, Rockville, MD. E-mail: probono@montgomerycountymd.gov.

Targeted selection/ placement procedures — don't limit pro bono volunteering to legal work. Think of various types of consulting services that might provide pro bono help.

Websites Connect With Pro Bono Consultants

Looking for pro bono consultants in your area? Check out these sources:

- ✓ Local chapters of various professional service provider associations
- ✓ http://catchafire.org/ (New York City area)
- ✓ www.taprootfoundation.org (San Francisco, CA; Chicago, IL; Los Angeles, CA: New York, NY; Washington D.C.)

47. Spell Out Expectations to Potential Recruits

It's important to eliminate any surprises when going over expectations with possible volunteers. Leave no room for misunderstandings.

See that the following questions are answered as fully as possible:

1. What are the exact work assignments?
2. How much time will be required on a daily, weekly or monthly basis?
3. Where should/can the assignments be carried out?
4. How many others will be involved in the assignment?
5. What is the time frame?
6. Who among the staff will serve as a resource or supervisor?
7. What type of training/orientation will be required?
8. What will be the outcome of the completed project(s)?
9. What are the volunteer benefits — both tangible and intangible?

48. Holiday Volunteer Description Details Role, Responsibilities

Recruiting volunteers over the holidays can be a challenging proposition. But spelling out a role's expected duties and requirements can help potential volunteers better manage their time during this busy season, and save the nonprofit numerous headaches.

Staff at Little Brothers-Friends of the Elderly (Omaha, NE) do this by describing the roles, expectations and details of holiday-specific volunteering positions in one concise form, which is distributed to potential volunteers. Monica Mora-Handlos, volunteer services coordinator, describes how this form has become instrumental when recruiting holiday volunteers:

How is this form used and how is it useful in obtaining volunteers?

"This form (shown right) is available on our website in the volunteer section. When volunteers give of their time, they want to know what will be expected of them, how much time they will need to invest and feel confidence in the organization they will be assisting. The volunteer description form provides potential volunteers with the purpose, the key responsibilities, location, time commitment, volunteer requirements and the benefits of volunteering for that opportunity."

How many additional holiday volunteers do you need to recruit each year?

"Little Brothers-Friends of the Elderly celebrates at least three holidays with our Old Friends including Easter, Thanksgiving and Christmas. We usually need to recruit a minimum of 50 new volunteers each year to assist with our holiday programs."

What tips could you share about creating a form such as this?

"It is vital for agencies to take the time to define each of their volunteer opportunities. It sends a message to volunteers that you believe their volunteer position is as important as a paid office position, when they read a job description for the volunteer opportunities. It also assists the agency to have realistic expectations for volunteers within a position and to be prepared ahead of the volunteer event."

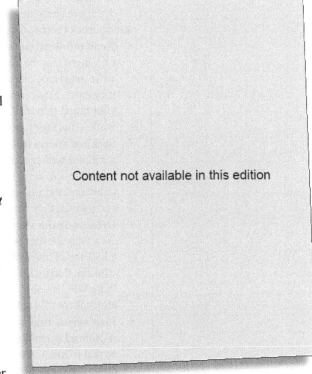

Content not available in this edition

Source: Monica Mora-Handlos, Volunteer Services Coordinator, Little Brothers-Friends of the Elderly, Omaha, NE. E-mail: mmorahandlos.oma@littlebrothers.org

49. Tips for Working With First-time Offender Youth Volunteers

Filling volunteer positions with youth seems like a natural extension for nonprofits, but working with first-time youth offenders may give some organizations reason for pause.

One group finding success working with this special population is Man in the Mirror (Casselberry, FL), a nonprofit Christian ministry organization.

Working with Florida's state Parole Alternatives for Youth (P.A.Y.) program, first-time offenders ages 14 to 22 fill data entry and warehouse positions alongside other youth volunteers in a school-sponsored Bright Futures program for high-achieving students to secure college scholarships. P.A.Y. volunteers work 20 to 40 hours over 90 days.

Employees are not told which students are from the offender program and which from the Bright Futures program, giving all youth the same footing.

Students must call on their own to interview for the position and may not have a parent do so, Mayer notes. Students who are accepted for the experience learn important career skills and can earn a letter of recommendation for future employment.

Source: Daphne Mayer, Volunteer Coordinator, Man in the Mirror, Casselberry, FL.
E-mail: daphnemayer@maninthemirror.org

50. Implement Strategies to Reach Out to Minorities

If your organization is seeking to gain greater support from minorities in your area — whether it is their time, services or financial support — there are a number of points and possible approaches to consider before you begin.

Start by identifying the specific minority groups to whom you want to reach out. Do some of your programs and services benefit these people? If so, might they be willing and able to become volunteers when they no longer require assistance?

Try these strategies to enlist help from minority groups, which will build your organization's track record of successful programs that fill a variety of community needs:

- **Read publications produced by minority groups.** Depending on the size of your city, there may be many newspapers, magazines, newsletters or even television and radio programs that will help you become familiar with specific concerns or needs that may exist. Explore possible mutually beneficial relationships between members of your target minority group and your programs. Some may be looking for assistance, while others may desire a volunteer opportunity.

- **Seek out successful persons for their input.** Every group of individuals who share a cultural background has leaders and spokespersons, many of whom are successful in business or civic roles. Ask them to help your organization in long-range planning to better serve minority youth, families or seniors. If your goals and philosophies are compatible, they may consider acting as advisors, volunteers or board members.

- **Determine the varying degrees of needs.** As in every population, there will be persons who are successful and prosperous, middle income or in need of assistance. Seek a balance of involvement among them — those who can make contributions, those who can donate time and those who need your help. The success and experiences of those who are able to contribute can inspire those who are receiving, and promote an atmosphere of dignity and cooperation for the entire organization.

- **Plan events that will be attractive to different cultures.** If your community has a significant population of a minority group, create festivals or other types of events that appeal to them. Ask minority leaders to help you with authenticity and accuracy — make the event a true celebration of diversity to appeal to all of your supporters.

- **Recognize the valuable perspective minorities can offer.** Remember that the world is getting smaller — we now speak of a global economy and overseas markets in business. The same applies to charitable organizations; if you are to grow and thrive, multicultural input will be essential to your growth and success.

51. Daily Bread Takes Volunteer Descriptions to the Next Level

More than 10,000 volunteers are an essential part of Daily Bread Food Bank's (Toronto, Ontario, Canada) workforce. Using a detailed job description provides incoming volunteers with a road map to success and a document that will help them determine if the position is aligned with their skills.

The current opening of Advocacy Support Worker is no exception to the detailed role descriptions (sample shown below) available at Daily Bread. This role description offers in-depth details of all aspects of the position, which enables the volunteer staff at Daily Bread to locate the best person for the position.

To provide transparency and identify the best individual for any given role, consider adding the following details to your volunteer role descriptions.

- **Hours:** Use the role description form to outline the hours required and the minimum commitment needed. Daily Bread's Advocacy Support Worker description details three to six hours per week and a three-month commitment.

- **Training:** Detail the required training needed to fulfill and succeed within the position, along with the number of hours and timing of the training involved. If training requires five evening sessions in a row, spell that out here to avoid unnecessary expenditure of time on the wrong candidate.

- **Position Purpose:** After providing a detailed overview of your organization and the volunteer role, drill down deeper by adding a specific section that details the position's purpose. Take time to outline how this role fits into the larger picture of your organization.

- **Duties:** Spell out specific duties for each position posted. Avoid glossing over any duties that will be required of the individual that may be deemed unappealing, as it's best to offer more details and find the right candidate for the role.

- **Skills/Qualifications:** Make sure to list any specialized needs or skills required for the volunteer role. Consider offering a training period which allows a volunteer candidate ample time to obtain the training needed, allowing more individuals to be eligible for the role.

Source: Alisha Coroa, Volunteer Coordinator, Daily Bread Food Bank, Toronto, Ontario, Canada.
E-mail: Alisha@dailybread.ca

Job descriptions help provide would-be volunteers with a road map of what's expected and how to proceed.

Content not available in this edition

52. Steps for Managing an Abundance of Skilled Volunteers

Oregon Public Broadcasting (OPB) of Portland, OR, relies on the assistance of 1,500 skilled volunteers each year to conduct its membership drives that attract hundreds of new members. For radio membership drives alone, 400 volunteers assist over seven to 10 days, while television drives typically require 80 to 100 volunteers.

Fortunately for OPB, more than enough people step up to volunteer. However, that creates a challenge in and of itself.

"We have a surplus of extremely highly skilled volunteers and don't have the ability to place them all in the types of positions that they would most desire," says Dana Mahoney, manager of volunteer resources. Skilled volunteers assist in producing the station's two radio programs and act as on-air hosts, as research project assistants, associate producers and more.

Mahoney shares steps OPB takes to manage this volunteer abundance as well as volunteers' expectations:

- **Develop and maintain transparency.** "We attempt to make our application process and volunteer program as transparent as possible in an effort to let potential volunteers know what to expect about their relationship with OPB. For example, on the OPB Web page about how to volunteer, in addition to outlining some ways that volunteers are involved, we make a point to say that no new volunteer positions are continually in development. We also note that each month we send out a listing of current volunteer opportunities to all active volunteers. Also, once persons complete a volunteer application, we let them know what kinds of positions have ongoing need and how to stay in the loop to hear about new roles as they are created.

    "For volunteers who have applied for a specific position that has been posted, we are very clear about how competitive the process is by saying things within our communications such as: 'OPB is lucky to have an abundance of highly qualified volunteers. For this reason, we have developed a process to ensure that all candidates are evaluated fairly and that the needs of the agency are met. Thank you for understanding that while we value your interest, we are not always able to respond in a more personal way.'"

- **Create a clear process for skilled volunteer opportunities in the recruitment phase.** "We post internally created volunteer positions and distribute them to our pool of active volunteers, including a description of the position along with questions posed for the volunteer, such as: 'What about this volunteer position at OPB interests you? What do you hope to gain from this experience? What experiences have you had that you think might make you successful in this position?' Then, interested candidates respond to express their interest, answer the position questions and, perhaps, send along a résumé. The volunteer resources department then gathers all the applicant information, adds some additional information from their records (such as number of years the volunteer has with the organization, number of hours served, prior volunteer roles at OPB, etc.) for the staff supervisor. The staff member reviews the candidates and determines whom they would like to interview and eventually whom they would like to place in the role."

- **Create a process for volunteers with specialized skills or for volunteers who suggest a role.** "We identify volunteers with a highly specialized skill in their application materials, and occasionally volunteers approach us with a very specific idea about what skills they would like to provide or learn, or an exact role or project they would like to contribute toward. When this happens, we write a skills overview about the volunteer and share it with staff members who might be interested in the candidate. This tends to work out quite well for more temporary or project-based roles that require advanced skills."

Source: Dana Mahoney, Manager of Volunteer Resources, Oregon Public Broadcasting, Portland, OR. E-mail: dmahoney@opb.org

It's wise to be prepared to deal with an overabundance of volunteers, especially when it means volunteers won't be placed in their most desired positions.

53. Services Help Simplify Volunteer Screening Process

Properly screening volunteers not only protects your organization and those it serves, it communicates to potential and current volunteers the responsibility of their role.

At Montefiore Medical Center (Bronx, NY), volunteer applicants are screened with the help of a service called VolunteerSelectPlus^{SM}, a nonprofit employee and volunteer background screening service of LexisNexis Company (Dayton OH).

With 800 volunteers, Margaret Hamer, director of volunteer and student services, says screenings are a great help. They pay $15 per volunteer applicant screening, which Hamer says provides access to the most comprehensive public records and proprietary databases available for volunteer screening.

Screening volunteers through the service requires a government photo identification with date of birth; Social Security card; and signed acknowledgement and consent form. Upon request, the screening service will conduct a national criminal background check, identity check and/or a sex offender background check.

Hamer says the service has helped identify applicants who had criminal backgrounds.

"Our goal is to find a suitable fit for the medical center and the volunteer applicant," she says. "We're particularly careful to identify those who have not fully disclosed all criminal background on their application, have entered false information or forged any signatures."

Montefiore's high volunteer volume requires staff members to process required background screening of new applicants weekly, she adds. Through the service, "The background check oftentimes is completed within 24 hours."

Source: Margaret Hamer, Director of Volunteer and Student Services, Montefiore Medical Center, Bronx, NY. E-mail: mhamer@montefiore.org

54. Got a Gut Feeling? Check References

Did you get a twinge when interviewing a recent volunteer? Follow your instincts and check references before bringing that volunteer on board.

Ask each new volunteer for a minimum of three references and call those contacts before assigning a position. As an added safety measure, ask your volunteers to provide a letter of reference or two from a teacher, colleague or community leader. Treat new volunteers as though they are applying for a position within your nonprofit.

If the references you were given aren't checking out or seem hesitant to offer a glowing reference, consider the following courses of action:

- If your instincts tell you something isn't quite right, conduct a deeper level of review with references. Ask how the reference knows the volunteer and how long they've been acquainted. Develop a follow-up round of questions to ask references in order to dig a bit deeper into the volunteer's past.

- Advise the volunteer of any negative remarks that were brought up and ask him or her to address each item. If you're satisfied with the responses, invite the volunteer to join your nonprofit on a probationary basis. Set a time for a review when the probationary time expires to evaluate performance and prepare a course of action going forward.

- Schedule probationary volunteers to work closely with a staff member or an experienced volunteer to eliminate the possibility of problems while serving clients. Once a track record is established, begin to offer the volunteer more responsibility and evaluate performance consistently for the first year.

55. Qualifying and Training Volunteer Chaplains

Volunteer chaplains play a major role in hospitals looking to comfort patients. This is no different at Rady Children's Hospital (San Diego, CA). With over 300 beds available for chaplain service, a well-organized volunteer program makes the work of the Pastoral Care Department possible. Given the vulnerable situation many patients are in, qualifying and nurturing the volunteer chaplains is of paramount importance.

At Rady, volunteer chaplains are clergy or lay leaders who are ordained, credentialed, appointed and trained by their respective religious bodies. These chaplains provide pastoral care on an interfaith basis. Proselytizing, evangelizing or recruiting members to a congregation is prohibited and considered unethical.

Chaplains interested in volunteering must submit an application online. If qualified, they are invited to an interview. Those selected to serve must pass a background check, drug screen and TB test prior to starting.

Volunteer chaplains must attend a mandatory training and orientation. They also have to complete the hospital's volunteer training program, which gives an overview of relevant policies and procedures. Clinical pastoral care is a ministry subspecialty and requires additional training. The Reverend John Breding heads up the program and explains what is covered in the training: "Chaplains are trained on crisis intervention so they know the proper way to respond in the most difficult moments. We also teach them how to conduct a visit. This training is important to equip them with the tools and skills needed to have a successful volunteering experience."

Make sure to have policies regarding diversity, ethics, applications, background checks and training, so that your volunteer chaplain program is able to do a remarkable job of comforting and encouraging those in need.

Source: Reverend John Breding, Rady Children's Hospital, San Diego, CA.

Targeted selection/ placement procedures — volunteer chaplains should be required to submit an application; be interviewed; pass a background check, drug and TB test; and go through extensive training prior to placement.

56. Criminal Background Check: One Organization's Process

The Georgetown Independent School District (Georgetown, Texas) has used a criminal history check form for several years. Every person who applies to work with their students as a volunteer must fill it out, even current school district employees.

"By completing our background check, we know they've gone through our steps to be cleared to volunteer on our campus," says Karen Dooley, assistant superintendent for human resources.

The district's volunteer background check form must be filled out online. They provide computers for people to come in and use, if they don't have a computer or Internet at home. Once the form is filled out the school district submits it directly to the Texas Department of Safety.

"Within minutes we get something back that says they're clear or that something is showing up." Dooley says volunteers are often parents, but parents can also be turned down to supervise kids. "I don't tell them they can't parent; I just let them know they can't be in charge of other children."

Dooley says based on peoples' criminal background checks, sometimes they'll be approved to volunteer, but prevented from doing specific things. "If someone comes up with a 'theft by check' on their record, I might call them in and make a determination that I am okay with them volunteering, but not dealing with money."

They have an open door policy, even for those they turn down. "When volunteers are denied and they want to talk about why, I will meet with them and explain to them that they don't meet the criteria for volunteering."

Source: Karen Dooley, Assistant Superintendent for Human Resources, Georgetown Independent School District, Georgetown, TX. E-mail: dooleyk@georgetownisd.org

Make background checks mandatory when volunteers are expected to work with a more vulnerable audience, in this case, students.

57. Intense Training Precedes Zoo Volunteer Assignments

At the Prospect Park Zoo (Brooklyn, NY), 36 education docents serve as volunteer educators, offering a new, unique element to members as well as to the volunteer program.

Due to the more involved nature of becoming an education docent, the training requirements are more intense for this volunteer group. Those persons who are accepted into the program can expect to attend weekly training sessions for approximately four months. These sessions cover topics such as conservation, biology and informal learning. Trained docents can then begin to offer member tours, manage discovery stations and help at special events.

Docent trainees are required to take a series of 10 to 12 classes, which include a volunteer basics class covering the history of the Prospect Park Zoo and the Wildlife Conservation Society; on-site volunteering; handling animal contact areas such as the zoo's barn, wallaby/kangaroo exhibit, and walk-through aviary; zoo safety; and interacting with the public.

Docents then go on to take classes in interpretation, including exhibit and biofact interpretation, conservation, animal chats, and tour leading; the final classes are in animal handling, which include weekly written protocol tests, handling practice, plus a final live animal encounter demonstration to pass.

"As for commitment, education docents are required to complete 120 hours per year, and are asked to volunteer on a regular schedule. Most volunteer one-half day per week, but many docents do much more," says Debbie Dieneman Keim, coordinator of volunteers. "We also offer docent meetings about eight to nine times per year, which include presentations from our director, the animal department and education department or field trips to other facilities. Animal handlers are required to attend two animal handling meetings per year and submit a negative TB test result before training and every year after that to maintain their handling status."

Dieneman Keim offers the following tips for developing a successful education docents or similar program at your nonprofit:

✓ Make these volunteers feel needed. "Our zoo could truly not function without our volunteers," she says. "We have areas in the zoo that must be monitored at all times (animal contact areas, our Animals in Art exhibit, and our Discovery Center), and our volunteers know we need them."

✓ Listen to their ideas and use their talents. "Many of our volunteers have done research for our animal fact sheets, created themed biofact carts, and created games or craft projects for special events, or trained to become sea lion feeding narrators."

✓ Keep in contact and share information. "Although we do not have a formal newsletter," she says, "I try to reach out to everyone with e-mail updates and chat with them when they are volunteering. Our zoo director, Denise McClean, is often around and willing to chat with volunteers, and that really makes them feel welcome."

✓ Give them a community. "Docent meetings bond the volunteer crew together," says Dieneman Keim. "Our animal handlers work in pairs, and develop themes for their presentations, which gives them ownership of their programs, and many new friends."

✓ Celebrate their accomplishments. Everyone loves praise, parties and a word of thanks. At the zoo, they have different levels of volunteering. The Discovery Guides and Discovery Center volunteers wear burgundy shirts and docents wear light blue shirts, the same color as the education deptartment's paid staff.

✓ Have a hook that makes you different. "Our animal handling program is extremely attractive to potential volunteers," she says. "They develop a real bond with the animals that keeps them coming back. After all, it is really all about the animals!"

Source: Debbie Dieneman Keim, Coordinator of Volunteers, Prospect Park Zoo, Brooklyn, NY. E-mail: ddieneman@wcs.org

Targeted selection/ placement procedures — because more is expected of them, docents deserve a higher level of training and education prior to beginning their work.

58. Provide Background Checks

If cost is stopping you from doing background checks on volunteers, consider newly available online resources such as those offered by MyBackgroundCheck.com (Redding, CA). Partnering with the National Council of Nonprofit Associations (NCNA), MyBackgroundCheck.com provides a complete risk management program to the nonprofit industry.

The company's Volunteer Tracking System tracks volunteers in a network-like system, offering a thorough, cost-efficient background check program.

Performing thorough background checks on volunteers allows nonprofit organizations to continue to operate with ethics and integrity, says Tim Delaney, NCNA president and CEO.

The risk management program features a denied parties list that identifies all volunteers found to have a criminal record or adverse behaviors reported by an organization. It also provides flexible packages and a timesaving Web interface to organize and track volunteer screening.

For more information, log on to www.pre-employ.com and click on the Volunteer Tracking System link.

59. Provide Positive, Structured Evaluations

Jane Merritt, director of volunteer services at William R. Sharpe Jr. Hospital (Weston, WV), offers a standard volunteer evaluation process with a positive twist, noting that managing volunteers with a positive approach aids in retention and overall morale.

"I developed a volunteer evaluation system, as I am a firm believer in evaluations as a positive tool to improve and not a negative to discourage," says Merritt. "Some of the volunteers come in off shifts, and I don't want to lose touch with them or make them feel I do not care. This keeps us in touch."

Here Merritt answers questions about her successful evaluation process:

What is the optimal time for a review of a new volunteer?

"I chose (after) one to two months because it seems enough time to have developed some ideas and understanding but not too much time to make them feel they are alone and unappreciated."

What are the most common types of problems your evaluation uncovers?

"It has most generally been positive suggestions or questions such as: 'Can I work more time than what I originally requested?' 'Are there other areas that I could volunteer in as well as where I started?' I did have one volunteer request to work in an office setting as opposed to with the patients as they felt uncomfortable. My No. 1 priority is our patients, so I need to know if a volunteer is uncomfortable because it can be detrimental to the patient."

What kinds of interventions can be taken to remedy issues that arise?

"I am always happy to increase a volunteer's hours if they request it. Also, some areas do not need as many hours at a time, so splitting the volunteer's hours between two departments is a win-win situation. When a volunteer is not comfortable with patients as mentioned above, I reassign them to an office setting. They continue to work many more hours in this setting, filing, typing, answering the phone and allowing the staff more time with patients."

Do volunteers in different kinds of settings or roles need different kinds of evaluations or is one general one sufficient?

"I find that my survey is generic enough to cover all of the different volunteer opportunities at this time. If at some point, it needs updating, it can be done easily. One procedure that I follow to measure and evaluate volunteers is to send a volunteer evaluation as well as an evaluation of the volunteer's service. I send one to the head of the department that the volunteer works under and one to the volunteer to evaluate what they are doing. I usually do this at the end of one to two months of service. This helps me improve the program and takes care of problems before they get out of hand."

Source: Jane Merritt, Director of Volunteer Services, William R. Sharpe Jr. Hospital, Weston, WV. E-mail: Jane.E.Merritt@wv.gov

Evaluations help to confirm that the best placement has occurred of if a change may be in order.

60. Stay Tuned In to Identify Volunteers' Life Cycles

One of the primary reasons volunteers agree to assist an organization is because they enjoy contributing their skills and knowledge for a worthwhile cause. But they also have a variety of reasons for choosing your particular institution, such as working with their friends, having more opportunities to be assigned to jobs they love to do and identifying strongly with your mission and purpose.

When the combination of these reasons are well balanced, volunteers may spend many years generously offering time and talents to your cause. But if these reasons change and they no longer feel a solid bond with the organization, their enthusiasm will likely weaken as well.

Because both your organization and individual volunteers are constantly active and evolving, changing or expanding in scope, a natural cycle of involvement typically exists between most organizations and their volunteers. Even if the volunteer naturally becomes less active, he/she will be able to pass the baton to a newer volunteer waiting for a chance to do the same work with a different approach.

Realizing that the natural life cycle of volunteering varies greatly from person to person, consider these approaches to keeping the flow moving in an orderly direction, which will help ensure more seamless transitions as changes inevitably occur within the structure of your volunteer team:

Recognizing the natural life cycle of various volunteer positions helps to create more seamless transitions.

- **Determine the length of service for key positions.** When you have an unusually talented group of volunteers together, ask if they would commit to a term of two to three years and train a replacement group during their last year. Your new group will have a strong background for their duties, and have time to see others in action that may be qualified to replace them. When lengths of service are predetermined, no one will be offended when it is time for them to take on a different assignment, and may even enjoy their duties more fully knowing that it won't be a lifetime commitment.
- **Communicate with volunteers who are especially valuable.** All volunteers are appreciated and highly valued, yet some stand out as gifted and innovative. They may have more than one skill to share, but still have difficulty finding a niche within your organization. Work as closely with them as possible, even offering a five-year plan with the combination of variety and consistency they seek as a volunteer.
- **Establish both long- and short-term responsibilities.** Some volunteer duties, such as chairmanships of major events, fall neatly into a one-time category. A past chairman can then become an advisory chairman or honorary chairman. But other assignments benefit from consistency and prior experience. Ask volunteers how they feel about doing the same job more than one year — they may be eager to serve a second time after having learned the ropes, or they will know the job is not right for them. Making the effort to accommodate either preference benefits both you and your volunteers, keeping them satisfied longer.
- **Find a place for both one-time and lifetime volunteers.** Depending on their individual personalities and skills, some volunteers will be straightforward about how long they intend to be involved with your organization. They may have career or family plans that affect their length of service, hope to make contacts in as many organizations as possible, or want to offer the same skill to more organizations rather than doing many jobs for just one. Graciously accept volunteer help on the volunteer's terms. One person offering expert assistance on a one-time basis when it is most needed can be as beneficial as years of service by a marginally enthusiastic lifetime member. Both types are valuable, but for different reasons.

When it has become clear that one of your volunteers has lost enthusiasm for your causes, no one is benefiting and efforts may even be impeded. Even though volunteer managers are sorry to see this happen, it may be only a natural part of that particular volunteer's life cycle with your organization. However, those individuals may be willing to continue to serve as an occasional advisor — asking them to consider this will leave the door open for them to return if they have a change of heart.

61. Volunteer Guidelines for College Students

Setting guidelines for your college-aged volunteers can help eliminate problems and make sure everyone is on the same page

Since 1985 Tiertza-Leah Schwartz has been the director of voluntary services at Smith College (North Hampton, MA). "When coming up with guidelines, it's important to keep the needs of the agencies in mind," she says. During her time in this position she has come up with a list of guidelines titled "Placement Guidelines/Suggested Best Practices" which she reviews with each of her student volunteers before sending them out on a job. "It's all about respect for the agencies. The guidelines help give a framework for the types of expectations these students must fulfill," says Schwartz.

The guidelines cover a variety of issues ranging from personal safety to maintaining a professional relationship. "Whether it's a long- or short-term project, these guidelines apply," she says. While Schwartz reviews the guidelines with students before they begin volunteering, the guidelines are also available for students to review online (see www.smith.edu/cso/directory.pdf, pages 10 - 12).

Source: Tiertza-Leah Scwhartz, Director of Voluntary Services, CSO Office, Smith College, North Hampton, MA. E-mail: TSCHWARTZ@smith.edu

62. Placement Questionnaire Addresses Volunteer Satisfaction

You and your staff invest plenty of time and resources into recruiting and training volunteers. But what do you do to measure their satisfaction levels or address concerns?

Volunteer services staff with Saint Joseph Hospital (Lexington, KY) use a one-page placement questionnaire to measure how satisfied new volunteers are with their assignments. Jamine Hamner, volunteer coordinator, says they developed the form six years ago after realizing they rarely saw many volunteers once they began volunteering, either because of the placement location or the volunteer's shift.

Hamner mails or e-mails the placement questionnaire, shown here, with a cover letter to volunteers two months into an assignment. She reviews responses and forwards them to the director or unit manager to which the volunteer is assigned.

"If a volunteer is not happy with his or her placement, we can notify the staff, so they can work with the volunteer to make the placement better, or we can reassign the volunteer to a more suitable placement," she says.

She estimates her office sends 300 questionnaires annually and sees about half returned, noting that the use of e-mail has resulted in a slight increase in returns.

Source: Jamine Hamner, Coordinator, Volunteer Services, Saint Joseph Hospital, Lexington, KY. E-mail: hamnerja@sjhlex.org

Content not available in this edition

63. Confirm Volunteer Assignments in Writing

What tools do you provide your volunteers to help them succeed?

As you work with multiple numbers of volunteers on projects requiring individualized follow-up, your odds of having them complete assigned tasks will improve significantly if you provide each volunteer with written confirmation of what it is he/she is supposed to do (and by when).

Whenever you conduct a meeting in which volunteers leave with agreed-to tasks, immediately send them a personalized memo — as opposed to a standardized group memo — confirming their duties. Spell out exactly what is expected of them, and include a deadline for the project (or multiple deadlines for portions of the project).

In addition to delineating each task, clearly state how to report back or turn in completed work. This helps bring closure to the task.

Here are two techniques you may want to include in your memo:

1. Offer an incentive for completing tasks on time.

2. Add a final sentence to your memo indicating that all persons not having completed their tasks by the stated deadline will be contacted by you (or the appropriate person) to determine what needs to happen in order to finish the project. Adding a closing statement such as this motivates volunteers to avoid the embarrassment of being contacted while, at the same time, provides you with a justifiable reason for following up with them.

Example of a memo confirming a volunteer's duties:

> *Help your volunteers get off on firm footing by sharing their assignments in writing.*

January 3, 2012

St. Joseph's Hospital
FOUNDATION

TO: Tom Peterson, Sponsorship Committee
FROM: Brenda M. Hawley, Sponsorship Chairperson
RE: Calls to Be Completed By February 15
CC: Debra M. Brown, Director of Alumni

Thank you, Tom, for attending the December 13 Sponsorship Committee meeting and agreeing to call on the following businesses to serve as sponsors for our upcoming event.

As you know, it's imperative that we have commitments from these businesses by February 15 if we are to remain on schedule with our event timeline. For that reason, I am suggesting you schedule appointments for this week and next so business owners and managers have sufficient time to make a decision.

Please turn in (or fax) your completed calls to the Office of Alumni as you complete them. The fax number is 465-9097. As was mentioned at our meeting, those who turn in all calls on time will receive two 50 percent off coupons for dinner at Winchester's.

I encourage you to call Debra Brown or myself if you have any questions, need any assistance or experience any difficulty that would impede your ability to complete these calls on schedule.

I will plan to contact any persons who have not turned in their calls to the Office of Alumni by February 15.

Thank you for your valuable assistance with this portion of our 2010 Celebrity Speaker Event.

<u>Sponsorship calls to be completed by Tom Peterson by February 15:</u>

- Benders Office Supply & Equipment
- Determan Pepsi Distributors
- Osborne Trucking, Inc.
- Klein Brokers
- Castrole Travel
- Peterson Photography
- MasterCuts
- Winston Raceway

64. Call Potential Volunteers

Whatever else your volunteer interview process may involve, make sure it includes a short phone interview. Though the press of work might tempt you to rely on less interactive screening processes, one quick conversation with each applicant can be a great way of indentifying unique and valuable skills for which you never would have thought to look.

65. Spell Out Volunteer Requirements to Save Time, Funds

Your ability to attract, place and manage large numbers of volunteers will improve by spelling out the requirements of each position in advance.

Spelling out volunteer requirements from the get-go is an important part of starting volunteers on the best footing. Officials at the UW Medicine Harborview Medical Center (Seattle, WA) have taken the time to spell out volunteer requirements on their website, detailing information on health screening, security screening, commitment, age, attendance, sign in and sign out, dress code and background checks.

With 450 to 500 volunteers to manage, Monica Singh, MPA assistant director of volunteer and community services, has found that putting the guidelines front and center is helpful for both the nonprofit and potential volunteers.

"Spelling out the volunteer requirements has been useful in that we have seen an increased rate of accurately completed volunteer applications," says Singh. "The requirements listed are determined by human resources, hospital compliance and privacy policies, process improvement initiatives, state requirements and general experience of working with volunteers."

One advantage of sharing these requirements has been a decrease in the processing time of volunteer applications.

"By clearly stating our requirements up front, volunteer staff spend less time calling volunteer applicants to mail or drop off another required form," she says. "In addition, fewer volunteer applications are mailed back for being incomplete."

This simple step has also had a number of other effects, including:

- Reducing mailing costs.
- Decreasing the number of office phone calls pertaining to specific questions.
- Freeing up volunteer services staff to work on other tasks and programs.
- Reducing misunderstandings and communication errors about basic applicant requirements.
- Speeding up application processing time, allowing volunteers to be interviewed more quickly and efficiently.

Source: Monica Singh, MPA, Assistant Director Volunteer & Community Services, UW Medicine Harborview Medical Center, Seattle, WA. E-mail: ms5@u.washington.edu

How to Create an Effective Volunteer Requirements List

Monica Singh, MPA, assistant director of volunteer and community services at UW Medicine Harborview Medical Center (Seattle, WA), shares tips for creating the most effective list of volunteer requirements:

- Hold a brainstorming session with your volunteer services employees. Include key hospital staff who have a vested interest in creating a volunteer program that supports the hospital's HR policies and compliance standards.

- As a team, make a list of all the requirements that a volunteer applicant must meet before he/she can start volunteering in the organization.

- Get input from all your key stakeholders, so they can provide their perspective and represent the organization's varied interests.

66. Criminal Disclosure Form Helps Protect the Vulnerable

When a volunteer is working closely with patients, children or vulnerable adults it helps put your mind at ease, knowing that person's criminal history. In some states certain laws have even been created requiring volunteers who work with vulnerable individuals to fill out a criminal disclosure form.

One example, where a criminal disclosure is required, is the state of Washington. That's why all volunteers at Highline Medical Center (Burien, WA) must fill out a criminal disclosure form.

Kimberly Couret, volunteer coordinator for the medical center, uses the information provided on the forms to then go to the Washington State Patrol website. The website provides criminal background information gathered by law enforcement agencies and courts throughout the state of Washington. "Our number one priority is to ensure a safe environment for our patients, staff and other volunteers. A criminal disclosure gives the applicant the opportunity to explain if they have had a criminal background. This explanation allows me some insight into the potential volunteer and whether they would or would not be a good fit for our institution," she says. Couret says there have been times an applicant has been denied as a volunteer based on certain felonies disclosed on these forms.

The state of Washington is one example where laws have been put into place to protect children or vulnerable adults. Washington laws RCW 43.43.834 and RCW 43.43.842 were created to specifically spell out the requirements for background checks for employees and volunteers who may have unsupervised access with these individuals. Since state laws can vary when it comes to what is legal when it comes to background checks, be sure to check with a lawyer or other expert on what the requirements are in your state.

Content not available in this edition

How to Keep Volunteers With a Criminal Past From Slipping Through the System

Requiring volunteer applicants to fill out a criminal disclosure form brings to your attention their criminal past. But how can you be sure they are telling the truth? Lynette Brown, Background Check Unit Supervisor with the Washington State Patrol (Olympia, WA), has these three suggestions for making sure someone with a criminal background doesn't slip through the interview process:

- Ask to see a valid picture I.D.
- Run a background check through your state patrol office or the department of public safety. Costs can vary from state to state. In Washington, for example, nonprofits can receive a free background check on potential employees/volunteers.
- Request a thumb print. Positive identification or non-identification can only be determined upon receipt of fingerprints. In Washington, for example, if you are doing a background check and come across a duplicate name/birthdate (e.g., two John Smith's both born on 3/21/76) a thumb print is required. If a thumb print is necessary, personally take the individual to the police department, so you are sure it is their thumb.

Source: Lynette Brown, Background Check Unit Supervisor, Washington State Patrol Identification and Criminal History Section, Olympia, WA. E-mail: lynette.brown@wsp.wa.gov

Lightning Source UK Ltd.
Milton Keynes UK
UKOW06f2122020913

216389UK00008B/202/P